coming together

Celebrations
for African American Families

By Harriette Cole and John Pinderhughes

Jump at the Sun
Hyperion Books for Children
New York

With great joy I offer my gratitude to the many generous hearts who have provided so much love and support to me since my first moments in this world. I cannot say enough about how much I appreciate family—my parents, Doris Freeland Cole and the late Harry Augustus Cole; my grandmothers, Carrie Freeland and Rosina Cole; my sisters, Susan Cole Hill and Stephanie Hill, and my extended family—what a bounty of continuous love. I am grateful to my husband, George Chinsee, for always being both my anchor and my launching pad. To the younger ones who continue to show me what spontaneous joy looks like—especially Kori-Morgan, Cole-Stephen, Cameron-Davis, Akilah, Brittany, and Andy—thank you for being purely you.

We are all part of such a profound legacy of love and strength. I offer my lifelong gratitude for those who have come before me, and those seen and unseen beings who continue to encourage us all to find meaningful ways to come together.

—Harriette Cole

I would like to thank my family for the loving and nurturing environment in which I was raised and continue to live. Special thanks to my wife, Victoria, and my daughters, Sienna and Ghenet, whose unconditional love and support have made it all possible. Thanks to the spirits of my people whose strength, courage, and humanity have served us all well.

—John Pinderhughes

For information address Jump at the Sun, 114 Fifth Avenue, New York, New York 10011-5690.

Printed in Singapore

First Edition
10 9 8 7 6 5 4 3

Library of Congress Cataloging-in-Publication Data
Cole, Harriette.
Coming together: celebrations for African American families: Christmas, Kwanzaa, family reunions, and naming ceremonies / by Harriette Cole and John Pinderhughes.
p. cm.
Includes index.
ISBN 0-7868-0753-9
1. African American families--Social life and customs. 2. African Americans--Social life and customs. 3. African Americans--Anniversaries, etc. 4. Family festivals--United States. 5. Holidays--United States. 6. United States--Social life and customs. I. Pinderhughes, John, 1946- II. Title.
E185.86.C5813 2003
306.8'089'96073--dc21
2003043848

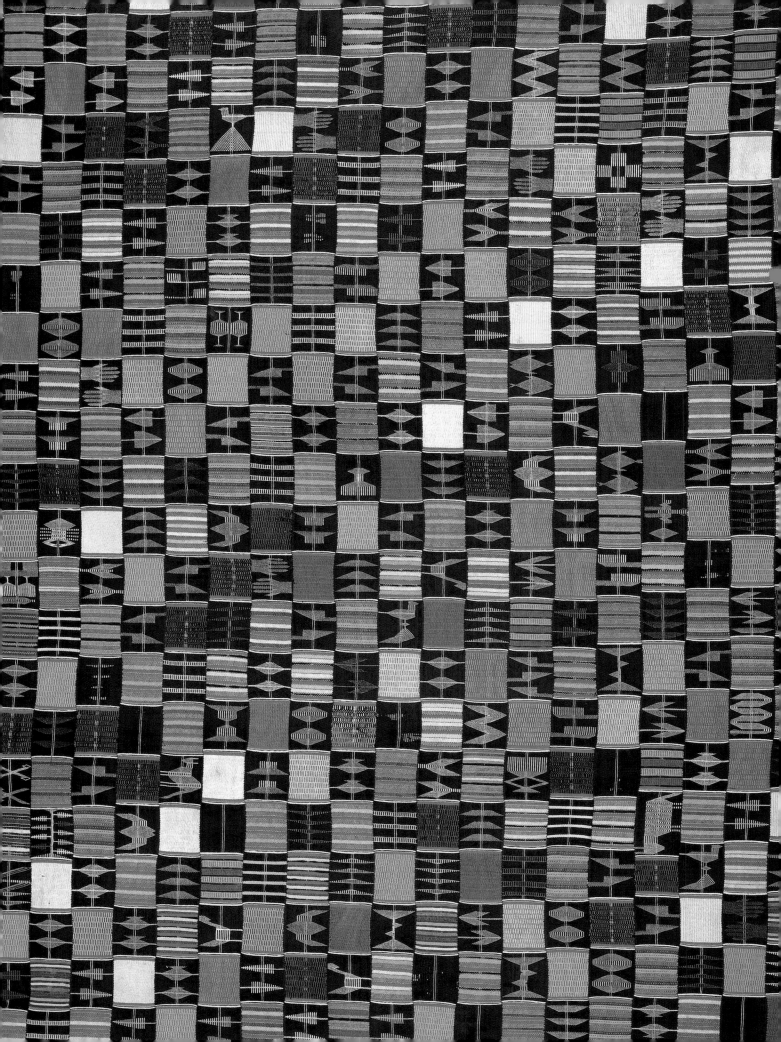

introduction

AFRICAN AMERICAN FAMILIES ARE DYNAMIC AND POWERFUL. WE HAVE SUPPORTED ONE another through struggle and triumph. We are famous for the extended family—grandparents, aunts and uncles, cousins—who help out whenever there's a need. For generations we have followed the wisdom born of our people's heritage: it takes a whole village to raise a child. It does take each one of us to pay attention to each other and show our love. These days many of us are so busy that we don't spend as much time together as we would like. We can change this. Indeed, we must. Every day there's something we can do to demonstrate how we care about one another. It may be sharing a meal together. For children it may mean telling your parents you love them every day when you wake up and before you go to bed. Or for those who no longer live at home, it's remembering to call and visit regularly. Writing notes to grandparents and elder relatives keeps them in our thoughts and prayers and lets them know what's going on in our lives. By practicing remembrance of our family members we can keep the fires of love burning brightly.

When it comes to special occasions, we can go all out as we come together in meaningful ways. This book is devoted to a few of the special occasions that many African American families honor. It's filled with ideas for how children, teenagers, and adults can team up to make the planning and execution of their celebrations meaningful for everyone.

The book evolved organically. John and I have been talking about our family activities for as long as we've known each other, some twenty years. At some point, John said: "Let's do a book about Kwanzaa, Harriette." To be honest, my first thought was, "No, thanks." My family gets together for lots of activities, but Kwanzaa hasn't been one of them. I didn't have anything against the celebration, but also I didn't have any personal affinity for it. John's query sparked my curiosity. Because I have always studied our culture, I knew the principles of Kwanzaa. I also knew that there had been significant controversy surrounding its evolution. Some African Americans have contended that Kwanzaa is a manufactured celebration, created in 1966 by Dr. Maulana Karenga, a black nationalist who has, over the years, been a subject of both controversy and acclaim. Others have dismissed it as a celebration of interest only to the small sector of our community who immerse themselves in African-centered philosophy, attire, and lifestyle.

John's invitation came as a surprise. John Pinderhughes, a celebrated photographer and chef from a large family of professionals, celebrates Kwanzaa. I realized that there had to be a reason for his embrace of this annual weeklong activity. So I took a deeper look at the meaning of Kwanzaa and the potential value that it can have for all of our lives. I'm glad I did. The principles that Kwanzaa's founder developed are designed to keep black families and communities strong—exactly what we need now.

Inspired by our initial discussions about Kwanzaa, our book idea expanded into a fuller look at how our families honor each other. As you will see, it is far broader than our original plan. We have created a book about some of the celebrations in which we participate with our family members and close friends. In the spirit of Kwanzaa, we have looked at a number of other key gatherings to see how we can come together and honor each other in tangible and intangible ways that celebrate our mutual love and respect. This book's intention is to include everyone in the celebration being explored—young and old, teens and middle-aged, toddlers and elders. Our goal is to illustrate how we can be together with the people we love the most and make each moment count. Yes, it requires slowing down in the midst of our busy lives to pay attention to what's going on around us, to make plans that include every person, to choose to celebrate the goodness and strength that live within us and those we love. Be mindful as you craft your gatherings and celebrations. And let every member of the family pitch in to help.

We can invigorate our families so that all of us stand strong and proud. May this book of celebrations inspire you to embrace those you love and appreciate them for all that they are bringing to the world! We offer it to you with our love.

—Harriette Cole

chapter one

kwanzaa

Reinforcing Our Cultural Heritage

THOUSANDS OF AFRICAN AMERICAN PEOPLE CELEBRATE KWANZAA EACH year from December 26 to January 1. This seven-day celebration is a cultural bonanza, an opportunity for families all over the country to come together to honor our rich heritage, a gathering designed to fortify us as we transition from one year to the next.

Kwanzaa, which means "first fruits" in Kiswahili, one of the most widely spoken East African languages, represents the harvest of our knowledge, wisdom, and capability. This celebration encourages families and loved ones to reach into our historical reserves and learn about our heroes and heroines, to discover important facts about our personal ancestors, and to take steps in the here and now to strengthen our values as a community.

Professor Maulana Karenga, a visionary in African American culture, conceived the holiday in 1966. Karenga wanted to create an activity that would inspire people of African descent to learn about our heritage and to discover new and different ways to support each other in our lives.

Why Celebrate Kwanzaa?

Some families have been celebrating Kwanzaa since it was first created. Others, who have always celebrated Christmas, question the value of participating in another week of celebration at this busy time of year. John Pinderhughes, my collaborator on this book, says he wasn't immediately attracted to Kwanzaa when he first learned about it years ago. It wasn't until he and his wife, Victoria, had their two daughters that Kwanzaa took on any personal meaning. John says, "We wanted to make sure that our girls understood their heritage. Kwanzaa seemed like the perfect solution. It is a holiday for us that directs the whole family to learn about who we are." For more than a decade he and his family have been participating in Kwanzaa celebrations.

We've heard similar stories time and time again as we've talked to families across the country. When children enter the picture, everything changes.

Children need to know about their heritage. Through Kwanzaa, children get to learn and create at once. Kwanzaa is for all people of African descent, no matter what their profession, religion, or ideology. It's a celebration for people of every age: you're never too young or old to be included. And people of other ethnic backgrounds are welcome too.

The Vision of Kwanzaa

Professor Karenga, the founder of Kwanzaa, is chair of the Department of Black Studies at California State University, Long Beach. Holding two Ph.D.'s, in political science and social ethics, Karenga has devoted his life to the fortification and sustenance of Black people. He studied African cultures for many years before developing the celebration of Kwanzaa, based on the philosophy of Kawaida, which he describes as "an ongoing synthesis of the best of African thought and

A Family Affair

Aissatou Bey-Grecia has been celebrating Kwanzaa ever since her children were born. Being fully immersed in African culture, Aissatou says she knew how important it was for her children to learn for themselves what a powerful heritage they were born into. From the time that her children were walking and talking, they were learning the principles of Kwanzaa and how to live them throughout the year. When it came time to prepare for the celebrations, everybody had a job—anything from helping to get the food ready to lighting the candles. Over the years, Aissatou and her friends and extended family have divided up their celebrations, traveling to different homes for each day of the Kwanzaa week.

Further, Aissatou has always thought nothing is more precious than her family. That means that all of the original African art that she has collected over the years she has displayed in her home for her children—and now grandchildren—to touch and see. Being in the company of the art offers the opportunity to share stories of different groups of African people and what their lives were like. During the holidays, Aissatou selects special sculptures to inspire conversations.

Lighting the kinara each day of Kwanzaa is a highlight of the weeklong festivities. Make it extra special by including the children in the actual lighting. Akhnaten Spencer-El, a young adult, supervises younger members of his family and friends who have come to a Kwanzaa gathering at his family's Harlem home.

practice in constant exchange with the world." During his period of study and contemplation he learned about the many ways that our African brothers and sisters living in the Motherland revere the land, respect their ancestors, and draw upon their cultural heritage for strength and guidance. Karenga created Kwanzaa based on the five fundamental activities of continental African "first fruits" celebrations: ingathering, reverence, commemoration, recommitment, and celebration. Here's how you can understand these activities:

- **Ingathering:** Essential during Kwanzaa is time for people to come together to strengthen their bonds.
- **Reverence:** Like many other celebrations, Kwanzaa is a time to thank the Creator for the many blessings we have received.
- **Commemoration:** During Kwanzaa, we take time out of our schedules to review our history and learn about those who have come before us as well as how we can incorporate their legacy into our lives today.
- **Recommitment:** As we approach a new year, we also take time to review our resolutions that include celebrating and remembering our heritage. We commit to strengthening our resolve to live to our best ability.
- **Celebration:** Finally, during Kwanzaa we rejoice and celebrate the harvest of blessings that have filled our lives.

For more information about Karenga, visit: www.theofficialkwanzaawebsite.org

Remember the Ancestors

In African families the people who came before are important, and those who figure prominently in our lives are not forgotten once they pass. You probably can think of family members right now whose stories are still passed down. In my family, somebody's always remembering Little Grandma, my mother's mother. This little lady, who stood less than five feet tall, had a huge presence. She devoted all of her 101 years to helping other people and teaching them how to be kind and strong. One memory that crops up at many family events is how Little Grandma used to tell my sisters and me about the value of working together— *Ujamaa*. She used to say, "Two sets of hands are better than one, girls." And she was right. Whenever we stood next to Little Grandma, helping to wash and dry dishes, we got the work done in no time at all. Plus, we got to listen to great stories about life when Grandma was growing up. I'll never forget her.

What's great about Kwanzaa is that it's a time when you are encouraged to remember all of the great people who have been part of your life. If you want to know more about your grandparents, ask your parents, aunts, and uncles. Share memories of cousins and great-uncles or other relatives. The best stories are the ones that give details about the things that your family's ancestors did that continue to inspire you today. Your memories may be funny or serious. All of them are welcome.

Know too that our ancestors don't end with our immediate family. As a people, all of those who came before us and whose memory would serve us well deserve to be invoked. You may recall the lady at your church who always helped those in greater need or the mailman who consistently shared a kind word. Maybe you want to recall a teacher whose wisdom has stayed with you over the years or a

Make setting up your Kwanzaa altar a family activity. Select a central place in your home where the altar can stay. Gather each evening to light the candles and share your collective wisdom. Give everyone a chance to participate.

dance instructor who enlightened you about the power of movement in African tradition. Feel free to dig deep into your memory bank and allow those dynamic stories of love and history to emerge.

Seven Special Candles

The seven candles of Kwanzaa, the *mishumaa saba*, serve to focus our attention on the principles and legacy of our people. Each *kinara*, the candleholder that we use, is filled with seven candles: three green, one black, and three red. The green candles stand for the earth that is the birthright of every human being and the future of our people. The red candles represent the blood of our foremothers and forefathers who gave their lives so that we would have greater opportunities and quality of life. The black candle reflects the power of all people of African descent to unite and stand firm in our beliefs and our culture.

The black candle is lit on the first day of Kwanzaa. Some families allow the youngest child to light the first candle. The male elder invokes a prayer, asking God to shower His blessings upon all gathered and upon all the ancestors. And then the black candle is lit.

Each subsequent evening, festivities begin with the lighting of the kinara. So, on the second night, the first candle will again be lit, followed by the farthest candle on the left—which is red. The next day, the furthest candle on the right—which is green—is added, until by the seventh day, all candles are lit together to signal the final celebration day of Kwanzaa.

Kwanzaa Essentials

No Kwanzaa celebration is complete without a few basic components. These are items that you will use to set up your Kwanzaa altar, the central place where you put all of the items that represent your celebration. On each of the seven days, you and your family will gather around this altar to light your candles and participate in the rituals that you adopt.

Years ago, families had to make every one of these Kwanzaa items, because they were very difficult to find. Of course, it's still a great practice to make these items. If you choose to purchase some of them, you're in luck. Many local vendors sell Kwanzaa items. Plus you can shop on the Internet (try www.meekwanzaakit.com or www.cobbala.com and KofiBear.com) or at Kwanzaa festivals when they come to your hometown. Here's what you need. The words are in the Kiswahili language, along with their translations:

> Bendera (ben-deh-rah): The flag inspired by Marcus Garvey, which bears the colors black (for our people), red (for our ongoing struggle), and green (for the possibilities in our future). Get creative with the use of your flag. You can hang it outside your home during the Kwanzaa season so that it can wave proudly, honoring the seven days. You can hang it above your Kwanzaa altar, too.
>
> Kikombe cha umoja (kee-kom-bay chah oo-moe-jah): The unity cup that symbolizes the essential strength inherent in coming together as a people. The family elder can pour a libation to the ancestors using the kikombe cha umoja. Also each family member can drink from the kikome cha umoja when special blessings are being offered.
>
> Kinara (kee-nah-rah): The candleholder, the symbol of our roots as African

Take out family photos and tell stories of those who have passed on.

Top: John's grandfather, Charles Lloyd Pinderhughes, who was the athletics coach at Dunbar High School in Washington, D.C., for more than fifty years.

Above: Carrie Elizabeth Alsup Freeland, my grandmother, fondly known as Little Grandma, at her one-hundredth-birthday party.

people. The kinara anchors the rituals held each day of Kwanzaa by being the holder of the light that radiates our collective power.

Mishumaa saba (mee-shoo-mah sah-bah): The seven candles representing the seven principles of honorable, conscious living that are the basis for Kwanzaa. As the celebrations build and grow, more candles are lit—one a day—symbolizing the power and strength of our people.

Mazao (mah-zah-oh): Crops, such as pumpkin, squash, and other root vegetables, which represent the fruits of our labor as a people and family.

Mkeka (mih-kay-kah): The straw mat, the symbol of our tradition and history as people of African descent. Learn to make your own *mkeka* mat on page 30.

Muhindi (moo-heen-dee): The ears of corn, representing the children in the family and the potential for future generations of strong family members. Select dried corn that's bursting with the season's colors.

Zawadi (zah-wah-dee): Gifts, which represent the love of parents for their children and the rewards that the children receive for living honorably, as well as the commitment on the part of the children to respect their family, to fulfill their duty and love with integrity, by being honest, getting good grades, and treating others well. For ideas on making zawadi with your family, see page 53.

Know Our Heroes and Heroines

In school, children learn about lots of great people who have helped to make the world a wonderful place. During Kwanzaa they can focus attention on the many great leaders from our own history who have paved the way for our success. Each day of Kwanzaa activities, children can take turns sharing stories of heroes and heroines from their town or from world history.

- **Write a play** that siblings and friends can enact that dramatizes the life of a great African American leader.
- **Make flash cards** with illustrations on one side and stories on the other and quiz siblings and friends about great leaders. Children will teach while also reinforcing their own knowledge. There are so many great people whose stories they can tell. Some lived generations ago; others offer their wisdom to us now.
- **Find stories of our heroes and heroines** by surfing the Web. Your local library will have many books and periodicals chock-full of great stories. Encourage children to research stories about their own family members. Here are a few leaders to get your research juices flowing:

The Honorable Marcus Garvey (1887–1940)

This great man was born in Jamaica in the West Indies, where he lived for many years before traveling to Europe and the United States. After studying the history of African peoples on the African continent and in the Americas, Garvey came to believe that it was not possible for us to be treated fairly or equally in the West. Garvey was instrumental in leading a "Back to Africa" movement, through the organization he founded in 1914, the Universal Negro Improvement Association. His efforts did not yield the great community on African shores that

Above: Crops for your Kwanzaa celebration can vary, based on availability and preference. Be sure to include the mazao, corn (pictured at top), along with the other items. *Opposite:* Lighting the kinara is a favorite family activity, as demonstrated by Al Cuyjet and his daughter Alyssa Cuyjet.

Research the stories of our heroes and heroines.

Clockwise from top left: The Honorable Marcus Garvey, Sojourner Truth, Malcolm X, Nat Turner, Hank Aaron, Harriet Tubman, and Paul Robeson.

he had dreamed of, but they did lay the foundation for many pan-African activities over the years.

Harriet Tubman (1820–1913)

Known as the Moses of our people, Harriet Tubman was a determined woman. Born into slavery, Tubman was destined to escape along what came to be known as the Underground Railroad, a safe-haven pathway to the North comprised of homes and people who assisted runaways to freedom. A brave woman, Tubman made nineteen trips along the Underground Railroad to free her family members and many others. She lived until the age of ninety-three, still working to help brothers and sisters to live free and fertile lives.

Sojourner Truth (1797–1883)

Born Isabella in 1797 in Ulster, New York, this woman lived to know both slavery and freedom. She was a wife, a mother, an abolitionist, and a women's-rights advocate. A religious woman, Sojourner Truth—the name she adopted in 1843—devoted her life to helping free enslaved Africans and unleash the bonds that shackled women during her day.

The Honorable Thurgood Marshall (1908–1993)

The son of a sleeping-car porter and great-grandson of an enslaved man, Marshall defeated all odds to become the first African American to be appointed to the highest court in the United States. He became a justice of the Supreme Court in 1967 and served his term honorably until his retirement at age eighty-two. Born in Baltimore, Maryland, Marshall practiced law, serving many years with the NAACP. Indeed, he was part of the team of attorneys who argued the 1954 Brown *v.* Board of Education case that overruled the racist "separate but equal" doctrine, which had been preventing black youth from receiving a proper education. Throughout his illustrious career, Marshall fought for the underprivileged, always putting the rights of the people foremost.

Nat Turner (1800–1831)

This man was a courageous Christian who led a revolt against slavery in Southampton, Virginia, in 1831. Thanks to a series of visions that he had starting in his youth, he believed that God wanted him to help free the enslaved people whose destiny mirrored his own. As a result of his inner urgings, Turner led the Southampton revolt, which resulted in the deaths of more than sixty white people. Turner and others were caught and hanged, and the "Black Codes," which made life very difficult for black people, were more harshly enforced. In the end, though, the numerous, ongoing revolts fueled the efforts to end slavery and inspire the potential for freedom among our people.

Ralph Ellison (1914–1994)

Arguably one of the greatest writers of the twentieth century, Ellison was a true philosopher who studied the lives of African American people and shared our stories with the world through his words. He is most famous for the 1952 novel *Invisible Man,* which portrays the plight of an African American man who cannot find peace in white society. Born in Oklahoma in 1914, Ellison was accomplished in many creative fields. He found his calling during the Harlem Renaissance, when so much black talent was flourishing in the midst of tremendous hardship and tension.

Paul Robeson (1898–1976)

Born in Princeton, New Jersey, the son of a former enslaved man who became a preacher, Robeson became a true renaissance man. He was highly educated and received a law degree from Columbia University. Yet he was unable to practice law, a blow that pushed him into the arts. From 1922 until his death in 1976, Robeson had a romantic courtship with the world of theater and film. He appeared in many great productions, including the musical *Show Boat* and in Shakespeare's *Othello*, both in London and on Broadway. Robeson was more than an artist. He was a man of conscience whose visit to the Soviet Union in 1934 and subsequent espousal of what were considered left-wing, Communist views, prompted the U.S. State Department to withdraw his passport. Robeson's life was troubled from that point on, even after the Supreme Court vindicated him later. Like many other great African Americans, he spent time abroad, returning home a few years before his death.

James Baldwin (1924–1987)

One of the most compelling writers of the twentieth century, Baldwin knew from an early age that writing was his calling. He published his first story in a church newspaper when he was twelve years old. Born in Harlem, New York, the son of a domestic worker, Baldwin grew up poor. During his youth he witnessed the challenges of the time and wrote about what resonated with him: personal identity, sexuality, and civil rights. Among his many works are the novels, *Go Tell It on the Mountain, Native Son*, and *The Fire Next Time*. Not feeling welcome in the United States, Baldwin became an expatriate in Paris, living there until shortly before his death.

Toni Morrison (1931–present)

Novelist Toni Morrison is a genuine visionary. Born Chloe Anthony Wofford, she is the second of four children, who all grew up in Loraine, Ohio. As a child, Morrison was interested in literature. She graduated from Howard University in 1953 with a B.A. in English, with a minor in Classics. Morrison received her Masters of Arts from Cornell in 1955 and began teaching at Howard in 1957. She has taught at Yale University, Bard College, Rutgers University, and Princeton University. In 1970, she began publishing her own work, with *The Bluest Eye*. Morrison has written numerous compelling novels that explore the interior life of complex characters, including *Sula, Song of Solomon,* and *Beloved*, which won the Pulitzer Prize in 1988. She won the Nobel Prize for Literature in 1993. Morrison currently teaches at Princeton University.

Shirley St. Hill Chisholm (1924–present)

When she stood up and announced her intention to run for president of the United States in 1972, Shirley Chisholm made history. She was the first woman to run for president. Born in Brooklyn to West Indian parents, Chisholm grew up in Barbados under the supervision of her grandmother and the tutelage of the British school system. Back in New York, in 1934 she attended the famous Girls High School in Brooklyn, graduating in 1942. From there she attended Brooklyn College and faced racism head-on. Rather than simply being rejected by a social club she and her friends wanted to join, Chisholm formed her own. She graduated in 1946 with honors, but essentially couldn't find a job. Finally, she was employed by the Mount Calvary Childcare Center in Harlem. She married Conrad Chisholm, a Jamaican man who worked as a private investigator, in 1949. Together, the two got involved in local politics. It was time to take politics to a new level when Shirley Chisholm ran for a state assembly seat in 1964. She won and served until 1968. Subsequently, she won and served two terms as a member of Congress. During her tenure she cofounded the National Organization for Women (NOW). In 1972, this brave woman ran for president. Though she did not win, her voice was heard worldwide, a voice of reason in a world that sorely needed a new view. Chisholm retired from politics in 1982. She continues to speak across the country about empowerment.

Leontyne Price (1927–present)

Hailing from Laurel, Mississippi, Mary Violet Leontyne Price grew up in the segregated South. From a young age, it was apparent that Price was musically talented. When it came time to pursue higher education, she attended Central State University in Wilberforce, Ohio, on scholarship. Price moved next to Juilliard to further her education in voice. In 1955, she made history by performing as the lead in NBC's production of Puccini's *Tosca*. Her performance in 1957 of Verdi's *Aida* sent her on a European tour. In the midst of segregation, Price excelled, debuting at the Metropolitan Opera in Verdi's *Il Trovatore*, followed by many roles around the world. Her performance at Lincoln Center in *Antony and Cleopatra* secured her a place as one of the world's great divas. Price went on to win eighteen Grammy awards, as well as a number of operatic and concert recordings. She retired in style by once again performing *Aida* at the Met in 1985.

Ben Carson (1951–present)

This brilliant doctor is proof that what people say about you doesn't have to define your destiny. Growing up in Detroit, Michigan, Carson believed that he was dumb. As a child he and his brother suffered in school, often bringing home failing grades. He also had violent tendencies that almost cost him his future. Thanks to his mother's decision to turn off the television and send her children to the library, Carson began to feed his interests and cultivate his ability to learn. Instead of failing, Carson went on to win academic scholarships to college and medical school. He now serves as director of pediatric neurosurgery at Johns Hopkins Hospital in Baltimore. In 1987, he made world history after successfully leading a medical team to separate conjoined twins. Carson continues to break ground in his field, finding ways to care for children who are debilitated by brain injuries. He has received numerous honors and awards for his work. Carson has also written several books, including *Gifted Hands,* his first.

Martin Luther King, Jr. (1929–1968)

One of the most significant leaders in contemporary history, Martin Luther King, Jr., was an advocate for human rights, civil rights, nonviolence, and freedom for humankind. Born in Atlanta, Georgia, King was a good student who was on the fast track to Morehouse College as a young man, at the same time that race relations were heating up in America. Following in his father's footsteps, King decided to become a minister at age eighteen. By nineteen, he had graduated from Morehouse with a B.A. in Sociology and was also ordained as a Baptist minister. While studying at Crozier Theological Seminary in Chester, Pennsylvania, King began to study the teachings of Mahatma Gandhi. King married Coretta Scott in 1953, the same year that bus boycotts and riots erupted in the South. It wasn't until 1955, when Rosa Parks refused to give up her seat on a city bus, that King became a nationally recognized figure of the civil rights struggle. Defending Parks pushed King into the center of the controversy. For

Some of our great leaders.

Top, left to right: Toni Morrison, Sidney Poitier, and Ralph Ellison

Middle: The Honorable Thurgood Marshall, Dr. Ben Carson, Martin Luther King, Jr.

Bottom: Shirley Chisholm, Zora Neale Hurston, and James Baldwin

the next thirteen years, Martin Luther King, Jr., raised a family of five children and led the nation on the road toward equality. During this period he stood in harm's way countless times, always believing that his faith and principles would see him through. His efforts helped to desegregate schools in the South, establish the Voting Rights Act of 1965, and bring awareness to the issues facing Blacks and others in this country. He led the March on Washington in 1968, when he delivered his "I've had a dream" speech. Not long after, King was assassinated. His work lives on through his widow, Coretta Scott King, his children, the King Institute in Atlanta, and the many who continue to live by the beliefs that he espoused.

Malcolm X (1925–1965)

Born Malcolm Little in Omaha, Nebraska, Malcolm X grew up in the heat of the civil rights movement. One of eight children, the son of a homemaker and a Baptist minister who supported Marcus Garvey, Little was reared in a home that nurtured his personal power. Indeed, his father's nationalism put the family in harm's way several times during Malcolm's youth, resulting in the burning of their home in Lansing, Michigan, in 1929. Eventually, the family broke up—after the father's death—and Malcolm and his siblings went to foster homes and orphanages. This did not deter this smart young man. He excelled in school, until he realized that his dream to be a lawyer was unrealistic in his society. After he dropped out of school, a downward spiral began that led to a seven-year prison sentence in 1946 for burglary charges. During his time in prison, Malcolm continued his education, ultimately converting to the Muslim religion under the leadership of the Honorable Elijah Muhammad. Upon his parole in 1952, Malcolm assumed the surname X and lived according to Muhammad's teachings. Working as a minister and national spokesperson for the Nation of Islam, Malcolm X's voice was heard nationwide and the Nation expanded vastly. While standing in support of Black people during the height of the civil rights tension, Malcolm X also married Betty Shabazz and eventually had six children (a set of twins was born after he died). When a rift between him and Muhammad led to a break with the Nation, peril loomed. After he went on a hajj, a pilgrimage to Mecca, Saudi Arabia, and discovered that he shared beliefs with people who did not look like him, tensions grew to an all-time high. After many threats on his life, Malcolm X was assassinated at the Audubon Ballroom in Harlem while giving a speech. He was slain by members of the Nation of Islam.

Hank Aaron (1934–present)

A child of the Great Depression, Henry "Hank" Aaron found ways to entertain himself that would guide his career into superstardom. Born in Mobile, Alabama, Aaron occupied his free time playing baseball. Well, sort of. He actually crafted his own ball out of tightly wound rags because his family couldn't afford to buy a real ball. Throughout his formative years, Aaron played ball—from fast-pitch softball to baseball on a sandlot team. Inspired by Jackie Robinson, the young Henry focused his efforts on playing ball as his life's work. Aaron would ultimately make history with the Atlanta Braves by becoming a member of the very elite career 3,000-hit club in 1970. Before his career ended, Aaron set the home run record at a total of 755 home runs.

Historical Web Sites

Research can be fun and easy if you've got a computer. Just go to your favorite

One way to celebrate Kwanzaa when you also celebrate Christmas is to design a tree using African American ornaments. Many families honor both holidays in this way, inviting family members to make their own ornaments to hang on the tree and purchasing handmade ornaments from local vendors.

search engine and punch in key words like *African American heroes* or *black inventors* or *black writers*. Or search by your hero's name.

- www.blackhistory.eb.com
- www.black-network.com
- www.afroamericankids.homestead.com
- www.Melanet.com/Kwanzaa
- www.afroam.com

Don't forget to research your own family and community heritage. Your loved ones' accomplishments are just as important as those of the people you learn about in school. Find out their stories. Then during Kwanzaa you can share anecdotes about the great things they did.

The Beauty of Zawadi

We all love to receive gifts from one another. There's a certain magic to the whole giving cycle. The intention behind gifts during Kwanzaa is that each one should count. Naturally, parents are the main givers during the holidays. What they give their children makes a huge difference. Rather than just buying whatever the favorite toy or video game is this year, parents who participate in Kwanzaa are encouraged to draw upon our heritage to inspire their children to learn and grow. Books are among the standard gifts. Reading opens a whole new world to children. And no matter how young or old they are, there's a great book out there for them. Plus, books are interactive gifts. Parents can read to their young children when they come home from work and before bed. Beginning readers can read aloud to their parents and siblings and then talk about the stories that the books share. Out of books come so many opportunities for creativity, from enacting stories through song and dance to writing original stories.

In addition to books, there are lots of great educational gifts that parents can give their children. Among them:

- Software that teaches writing or math
- Clothing for school that reflects the intention and value of education
- Art supplies that children can use for expressing their own creativity
- Videotapes of African American stories
- Photographs of great African leaders
- Fine art with an accompanying biography of the artist

Zawadi are not just for parents to give to children. Kwanzaa offers the opportunity for children to create or buy gifts for their parents as well as the many other loved ones who fill their lives. In the spirit of Kwanzaa, children can use their imaginations and their hands to create Kwanzaa gifts. Writers can paint their poetry onto scrolls. Artists can draw pictures that illustrate family life. Bakers can whip up delicious cookies and cakes to share with everyone. See "Family Celebration Recipes" for desserts you can make together. Chemists can make candles and perfumes, with their parents' supervision. The whole family can get involved in making gifts for friends and relatives. Let your imagination be your guide!

Attend a Kwanzaa Extravaganza

The Drum and Spirit of Africa Society in Harlem, run by Obara Wali Rahman, hosts a fabulous event every year in honor of Kwanzaa. As the drummers invoke the presence of the ancestors and enliven the space, the event becomes vibrant and exciting for everyone gathered. Local vendors sell their wares, especially accessories and small gift items that make perfect zawadi. The children's African dance troupe performs an ensemble they've been practicing all year. And members of the community make a potluck meal.

In most cities across the country, cultural organizations stage special events during the season. Youth organizations host plays and art shows. Libraries sponsor book readings and signings by renowned authors. Art galleries and museums have special Kwanzaa art shows. And local community organizations host Kwanzaa events where many vendors sell their wares, as guest speakers appear to share their wisdom. Check your community listings for activities that will be suitable for the whole family.

Wear Festive Dress

Kwanzaa marks a dress-up occasion for every member of the family. Traditionally, people wear African-style clothing. Women often wear full tops with wrap skirts, which are called *lappas.* Men wear similar full tops with drawstring pants. They are known as *bubahs* or *grand bubahs* when they are made of extra-fine hand-loomed fabrics. Women often wrap their heads in traditional African cloth that complements or matches their outfits, in what is called a *gele.* Men wear crown-style hats, called *kufi,* which match their outfits.

Because African-inspired fashion has become so popular, the choices are broader now. Some designers use African textiles in Western styles. Others add inspiration to classic Western silhouettes, such as a strip of hand-loomed Ghanaian *kente* cloth, on vests for men and the bodices of dresses for women. Even if you don't choose to wear African-style clothing, you can accent your outfit with African accessories. Cowrie shells are the most popular as earrings, on bracelets, and necklaces.

If you want to get in the holiday spirit by wearing African clothing, consider your options. Make an outfit or purchase one from an African vendor in your town. Lots of companies make them in all sizes, from infant all the way to adult.

Be sure to have somebody take a picture of your whole group before the Kwanzaa meal. What a sight it is to behold a family all dressed up in their finest, paying tribute to the legacy that has brought us to where we are today.

Decorate with Style

We are visual people who love to celebrate our beliefs in our decor. This holds true during the Kwanzaa season. You may want to stay in the Kwanzaa palate that uses red, black, and green as foundation colors. Red and green are also popular Christmas colors, so if you also celebrate Christmas, your ornamentation may naturally flow into Kwanzaa. Feel free to add other elements too, such as metallics like silver or gold, to make the environment more festive.

Young people can participate in the decorations by making objects that celebrate family ancestors or African American heroes and heroines. To do this all year long, you can collect pictures from magazines and newspapers of African Americans who are celebrated, and frame them for the occasion. Children can

Design a Kwanzaa Tree

When Bebe Granger and her family began celebrating Kwanzaa at their home on Long Island, New York, a few years ago, they had to figure out how to incorporate this holiday into the huge Christmas celebration that had been part of their lives for years. Bebe decided to add a Kwanzaa tree to their decorations. Already her family erected a huge Christmas tree with ornaments that they have collected over the years, as well as homemade crafts that they add each holiday season. It was natural to add a tree that celebrated this "first fruits" holiday. What they did was to get a smaller tree and to decorate it with ornaments that celebrate African American life. All of the figures are brown skinned, some that they have bought over the years and others that they have created themselves.

Obara Wali Rahman, head of the Drum and Spirit of Africa Society, has devoted many years to teaching young and old to invoke the power of our heritage through music and dance. Research similar support where you live.

also ask their parents to pull out old family photos that can be placed on a mantel or other special area of your home. You can design garlands with banners that state each of the Kwanzaa principles, or make table runners and doilies out of African cloth, such as kente or *asooke*. Some vendors carry African-style cloth in cotton reproductions, so you can also buy yardage to make napkins and place mats for the *karamu* feast on the final night of the holiday (see "The Great Feast: Kwanzaa Karamu," page 26).

Nguzo Saba Day by Day

Kwanzaa is based on seven life principles. Families devote each day of the weeklong celebration to a particular principle, so that everyone can focus on that principle and bring its meaning to life.

Day One: Umoja (Unity)

People of African descent represent a large portion of the world's population. On this first day of Kwanzaa, take time to contemplate the meaning of joining together with your African family, friends, and neighbors.

Day Two: Kujichagulia (Self-determination)

On this day, we celebrate personal determination, because it is through this great quality that we become strong. When we strengthen our own will to succeed and be of value in the world, everything becomes possible.

Day Three: Ujima (Collective Work and Responsibility)

Little Grandma, my maternal grandmother, used to repeat all the time, "You don't do anything by yourself, girls." She was right. Even when we don't realize it, somebody else is helping us to get to where we're going. On this day, we pay attention to the importance of working together with others to make our dreams come true. By working together and sharing responsibility with others, we will find that everything is easier even as the reward is that much sweeter.

Day Four: Ujamaa (Cooperative Economics)

You've heard the saying, "Money is power." Well, in our society this is true. On this precious day of Kwanzaa, let's hold onto our economic power. As we learn on day four, working together can make miracles come true. When we recycle our dollars within our community and work together to build our businesses, we grow our power. In this way, we are able to take care of each other now and in the future.

Day Five: Nia (Purpose)

Start your day with a clear and focused intention. Before you get out of bed, ask the Lord to bless you with a clear purpose that can guide your steps throughout the day. Ask yourself, "What is my purpose for this day? What is my purpose for my life?" Hold on to these questions as you go about your day. You'll be surprised at the answers you get.

Day Six: Kuumba (Creativity)

Today is an exciting day. Today you are free to dream big. What does your imagination have in store for you today? How can you express your creativity? With so much focus all week on paying attention and working together, now you have the chance to allow all of that to soak in as your creative energy bursts forth. What will you create today?

Children dance in the annual Kwanzaa festival in Harlem, produced by the Drum and Spirit of Africa Society. The West African drum resonates throughout the space, infusing the dancers and all in attendance with its vibrations. Before the dance is done, everyone present is invited to join in.

Day Seven: Imani (Faith)

Nothing is possible without faith. Faith can be your guiding light. Faith that God will take care of you. Faith that your family will love you. And, most important, faith in yourself, the belief that you are capable of being the biggest, brightest star in the universe: a star who invites all the other stars to join in forming a magnificent constellation that celebrates who you are!

Nguzo Saba Exercises

There are many ways to honor each of the principles of Kwanzaa. To get started, we've come up with some ideas for each day. To make the most of these ideas, create a journal and record your progress.

Day 1: Celebrate Umoja (Unity)

To inspire your family to think unified thoughts, work on a project together as a team. It may be a community project that supports other people that you devise or that's already underway or a fund-raiser for your spiritual community.

Stop, look, and listen. Then write. . . . Go outside with your family to a favorite place in your neighborhood where people gather. It could be the local shopping mall. Maybe it's the park where mothers gather to watch their children play.

- Go there and make a vow to be silent for a few minutes and look around. Pay attention. What do you see? Who is there? What are the people doing? Do you see a connection in the people around you? Are you interested in any of the people?
- Do you notice any links between you and those around you? Look for similarities. Notice what stands out that brings all of you together. Look for the unity.
- Now go home and write about what you saw and heard. Emphasize Umoja in your journaling. What did you notice about the people that inspired thoughts of unity?
- Let your thoughts come out fluidly on paper, be it a poem or a picture. Let your vision of the principle of Umoja emerge.

Day 2: Kujichagulia Exercise (Self-determination)

This is the moment to work on making yourself a better person. Begin by examining your life and making a New Year's resolution you believe you can keep. Be specific and simple with your ideas, so that you come up with something you can fulfill in the year to come. For example, you may want to become proficient at a sport or write poetry or pay more attention to your family each week.

Write down at least one thing that really matters to you. Now figure out five things you can do to support what you wrote down. For example, an older family member may mean the world to you. To support him or her, you can:

- Visit once a week for at least an hour each time.
- Make art projects that can be framed and hung.
- Write stories about your relationship with this special person and share them when you visit.

- Give your loved one a hug and a kiss every time you see him or her to show how much you love the person.
- Remember to listen and appreciate his or her wisdom and apply what you hear to your life each day.
- You may discover that as you honor people and all that they mean to you, your determination to give your all will inspire you to give to others.

Day 3: Ujima (Collective Work and Responsibility)

Today's the day to go out and help somebody. You can work on a project that's already happening at your spiritual home, workplace, or school. Be aware of what's going on in your neighborhood. The whole family can work together to improve the lives of senior citizens in your community. You can work in a soup kitchen one day a week, deliver meals to the homebound, write letters to the elderly or homebound, help them pay their bills, or collect clothes that you mend and give to shelters.

Day 4: Ujamaa (Cooperative Economics)

Not everybody has time or patience to make Kwanzaa treats. But with a cooperative effort and a little ingenuity, family and friends create a world of Kwanzaa goodies. Your loved ones may like to design items made with cowrie shells, which represent abundance. Purchase your shells and other raw materials, such as string and African-printed cloth. Cowrie shells make very nice necklaces. Or, using shells and fabric, make change purses for men and women that remind your loved ones to respect our resources and share them with one another.

   You can also think about the future. Start a family investment club to set savings goals to work toward. Begin a college tuition fund with your investment club, so the entire family can work together toward making sure everybody gets a college education.

Day 5: Nia (Purpose)

Human birth is sacred. We were born with the ability to think and act based upon our own knowledge and will. When we live our lives with clear purpose, we support the efforts of our parents and other loved ones who came before us. Sometimes young people aren't always clear about their purpose—why they are here on the planet and what they are supposed to do with their lives. Everyone can benefit from a bit of introspection.

   To become clear, you can meditate. Sit quietly and ask yourself, "Why am I here? What am I supposed to do in my life?" Listen patiently for an answer. You may be surprised by how naturally inspiration comes to you when you ask for it. Maybe you will discover that today your purpose is to complete all of your outstanding responsibilities so that you can be free of worry or debt. Perhaps you will learn that you should study history or art, or that you should teach others what you have already learned. You may hear a voice within that tells you to walk in your grandfather's footsteps or to write a poem. Whatever comes to you, let that serve as your purpose for the day. If you begin each day with the resolution to refresh your purpose and stand firmly in it, your steps will be guided to your own great destiny.

Day 6: Kuumba (Creativity)

People of African descent are among the most creative in the world. African Americans have produced so many inventions that make our world run more

easily. George Washington Carver invented peanut butter and more than 300 products derived from peanuts, soybeans, and sweet potatoes. Elijah McCoy invented a lubricator for steam engines, and Charles Drew invented a way to preserve blood plasma. Our writers and philosophers, such as W.E.B. DuBois and Zora Neale Hurston, have filled libraries and minds with ideas for discussion. And our religious leaders, including Howard Thurman and Bishop Vashti McKenzie, have led us to greater understanding of spirituality.

You have a calling too. Know that you are in powerful company as you exercise your creativity. What's more, you are part of a community that welcomes your great efforts. So, what might your calling be? Can you sew? Draw? Make music? Design flower arrangements? Craft family outings? Don't be shy. Think about what you're good at doing and explore that. This is your day.

Day 7: Imani (Faith)

Our foremothers and forefathers have always known it. We do nothing without the support of the Creator. It is through the guidance and will of the one most High that we exist, and through the Creator's blessings that we experience triumph and loss. Practice having faith in that great power that guides and supports the Universe.

Especially during times of need, take refuge in your faith. During this season you can do this by attending a spiritual service with your family. You can gather at your Kwanzaa altar and make prayers as a family, asking for blessings for greater understanding. You may also want to make prayer sticks in the form of African symbols. Distribute the prayer sticks to your family members. Then write your prayers on the sticks and place them on your *mkeka* mat with your other Kwanzaa items. On the last day of Kwanzaa, read your prayers aloud to one another and then burn them in a sacrificial fire—making them an offering of love to the Creator.

The Day of Meditation (Siku ya Taamuli)

The final day of Kwanzaa also marks the first day of the New Year. As we know, on this auspicious day, it is common practice to assess your life and make a commitment to guide your steps during the year. In the tradition of Kwanzaa, this day is both one of great celebration and of tremendous contemplation.

Take a few minutes as your day begins and sit quietly for meditation. The questions that Karenga put forth to contemplate on this day of meditation are: Who am I? Am I really who I say I am? Am I all I ought to be?

Ask yourself these questions in the context of your life today. No matter how old you are, you can do this. A great activity is next to write down your thoughts and inspirations. Be sure to include everyone, including young children. From the first moments of life, as soon as thinking begins, we ponder the question "Who am I?" To consider it as a person of African descent in the twenty-first century is a great contemplation. You may want to take some time during your celebration on this last day of Kwanzaa to share what came up for each member of your family. You may collectively come up with a commitment for the year that will strengthen your personal resolve as well as your focused involvement in your community.

The Great Feast: Kwanzaa Karamu

Each night of Kwanzaa you can share special food with family and others who

When children gather, parents can spark a creative discussion by asking them to talk among themselves about what they want to do in their lives. "What do you want to be when you grow up?" is a great prompt. As they talk together, the inspiration will pour forth.

have come to celebrate. On the last day, however, it's time to throw down. The *karamu*, or feast, is the culmination of the week. Like other special-event meals, the karamu calls for the best recipes the family has to offer, the finest decorations on the table, and the longest guest list.

Many people celebrate the last day of Kwanzaa—which is also the first day of the New Year—by inviting other families to join the festivities. You can do this in a number of ways. Your family can host everything and simply invite others to attend. You may want to create a potluck meal where all of the great cooks who are invited prepare a special dish. What's important is to design a meal that incorporates exactly what you want and need to whet the appetites of all who will gather.

Introduce Others to the Celebration

John Pinderhughes and his family have been inviting people over for a karamu feast for years. They host their celebration at their home in Sag Harbor, Long Island, where there's a tight-knit community of black folks who enjoy spending quality time together. Many of John and Victoria's friends had never celebrated Kwanzaa before coming to their feast. What many have shared over the years is that they have such a full experience that they then want to be a part of Kwanzaa activities. Not only is the feast a delectable treat (after all, John is a seasoned chef who constantly dazzles the taste buds), but also the evening marks a time when people tell stories about their loved ones and share inspiration from what they know and love about our people. What John and Victoria affirm is that Kwanzaa is the season to share the richness of our heritage with those they love.

Make Space for the Generations

Grandparents love to spend time with their grandchildren. In some families, they get together frequently. In others, long distances make time together even more precious because it's rare. During the Kwanzaa season, be sure to carve out time when young and old enjoy each other.

You can host a sing-along during which you sing familiar songs or make up new lyrics. Why not use this as a great storytelling opportunity where Grandma enlightens young people with stories of how life used to be. And young people chime in with their own stories of how they are living their lives now.

Be sure to document these great moments on video and with still pictures. Later you can send copies of the photos to everyone in the family, with little messages of love from the children.

Write and Perform a Kwanzaa Play

In the spirit of creativity, organize a playwriting session with all the young people in the family. You may want to illustrate the seven principles of Kwanzaa where there are seven actors, each representing a principle. Your play can demonstrate how the principles can come to life. By incorporating an antagonistic character, you can also depict the value of choosing to practice the principles of Kwanzaa rather than succumbing to commercialism or forgetting about your heritage. Think about historic figures as well as people in your own community who would serve as great characters.

Once you have figured out your play, make costumes that reflect each of the characters. Then invite your loved ones to attend your special Kwanzaa

Drinking from the unity cup, the *kikombe cha umoja*, shows your reverence for the ancestors and your respect for one another. You can put water or juice in the cup, or even a special drink that you make together as a family.

Teen Time: Kwanzaa Party Ideas

Everybody can have a great and meaningful time during this season. For teens, that means it's time to be creative. Hosting a tea party can be a great idea.

The cost of entry can be to bring a handmade gift. The next day your whole group can take the basketful of gifts to a retirement home to give to the elderly.

During the party, you can divide up in groups and play a Kwanzaa version of charades, in which each person has to act out a different principle or famous African American hero or heroine.

Together write a song that you choreograph on the spot. You can perform the song the next day when you distribute your goodies.

After the fun and games, you can turn on the music and dance the evening away!

performance. Set up the space so that everybody can see and so that you have a clearly marked stage. You can do this in a basement or any other large open area.

Plan Your Kwanza Karamu Program

Plan your karamu carefully in advance to be sure everyone is included and the day goes smoothly.

Welcoming Guests into Your Home: Kukaribisha

Children can stand with their parents or teens to greet guests as they arrive. The standard Kwanzaa greeting is *"Habari gani!"* which means "What's the news of the day? What's happening?" The response should be the principle of that day of the week, such as "Nia" or "Ujamaa."

Acknowledgment of Elders

Anyone who is an honored guest at your festivities should be given special acknowledgment. This includes a comfortable seat in a place where all activities can be viewed, as well as an introduction to the group gathered. Give time for these distinguished loved ones to say a few words to everyone.

Creative Expression

Perhaps the children have written a poem or song or even composed a short play. Now is the time to present one of these treasures to the group. The focus of this moment should be Umoja, or Unity, the first principle of Kwanzaa.

Recitation of the Nguzo Saba, the Seven Principles

If there are enough young people present, each one can take a principle. The child can state the principle with its English translation and then describe what it means for African American people and for them specifically.

Words of Wisdom

No celebration is complete without words of inspiration to support and uplift those gathered. Invite a distinguished family member or friend who is well versed in the history of our people and who speaks well to share some wisdom. Talk to this person in advance and recommend a time frame, so that you keep the pace of the event flowing.

The Unity Cup: Kikombe cha Umoja

Being together during Kwanzaa symbolizes the potential for our coming together each and every day in our hearts and minds. The person officiating the event or a male elder can fill the Unity Cup with water or juice and offer a prayer. During the prayer he holds the cup in the four directions—north, south, east, and west. The cup is passed for all to sip from after the prayer and during the acknowledgment of the ancestors.

Honor the Ancestors and Call Their Names: Kutoa Majina and Kukumbuka

Each person in attendance has memories of someone who has passed on. The officiate can first make an affirmation that acknowledges all of the ancestors and their merits. Then you can go around the room and invite each person to call out the names of loved ones they want to remember. If you like, you can state one great quality about each ancestor that you want to remember. Following the affirmations, you can pass the Unity Cup.

Invocation of the Ancestors

Our African brothers and sisters advise us never to underestimate the power of the ancestors. When our loved ones pass on, they remain in our hearts and, as many will attest, they sometimes come to us in our dreams and in times of need. During this great occasion, you can invoke their presence through the playing of drums. During one Kwanzaa celebration, a four-year-old boy climbed up on a chair and just started pounding his drum in a perfectly artful way. Spontaneously, those surrounding him called out their ancestors' names together, which created an exquisite throbbing pulsation of sound. Later, some explained that they felt the presence of their loved ones in the room.

Karamu

Let the feast begin. Make sure that your table is set and that everything is ready. Whoever is going to help move things along should know in advance. People will be hungry now and excited to be a part of this great feast. To make an official start to the meal, have someone offer a blessing that inspires the spirit of gratitude and unity that Kwanzaa inspires.

Creative Expression

Endings are so important. When people are beginning their dessert is a perfect time for the young people to come back and offer another creative treat. Do you have a story about Africa? It could be from family travels or books you've read. Do you have a poem or reading that captures the essence of the family gathering? This creative exercise can serve as a moment that seals the love that's filling the room.

Farewell Statement: Tamshi la Tutaonana

Once again, a respected family member or friend comes forth to thank everyone for gathering. In a brief statement, the meaning of Kwanzaa can be restated and the power of living its principles in daily life reinforced.

Nurture One Another

The writer Sobonfu Somé speaks about the importance of being in a nurturing community in her book, *The Spirit of Intimacy* (Quill, 2000). She says that in her hometown in Burkina Faso, West Africa, one of the great roles of the village is to encourage the villagers to share their creativity so that they can discover their life's work and passions. Only when there is a nurturing environment, Somé explains, can one feel confident enough to be truly creative.

During Kwanzaa and throughout the year, remember to support your loved ones' creative efforts. Pay attention to each other. Be there to welcome the new ideas that are constantly bursting forth. Also, practice finding your own creative spirit and learning how to express and share your gifts with those who love and support you.

Kwanzaa Karamu

Plantain Chips

Black-Eyed Pea Fritters (Akara)

Avocado and Ginger Salad

Black-Eyed Pea and Rice Salad

West African Groundnut Stew

Baked Stuffed Fish Supreme

Classic Macaroni and Cheese

South Side Okra and Tomatoes

Aunt M's Peach Cobbler

Ginger Fried Bananas

Tropical Sorrel Punch

Let Creativity Reign!

Kwanzaa preparations are as important as the actual week of celebration. During the days leading up to Kwanzaa, you and your family can make zawadi. As well, you can make decorations and invitations and other items that will support your celebratory week. You may already be brimming with creative ideas. Here are some crafts with clear directions that the whole family can work on together.

Craft: Design Karamu Invitations

Although word of mouth is a traditional African way to let folks know about your celebration, a written invitation is a great option. This is especially true if you design it yourself. You may want to hand deliver the invitations to keep the personal touch.

What You Need

- Construction paper or colored oak tag (a type of board that is sturdier than cardboard, available at art-supply stores)
- Red, black, and green markers
- Glue
- Scissors
- African symbols (look in books you have or go online to find ideas)
- Cowrie shells or beads (optional)
- White paper to practice

Getting Started

1. Organize the particulars of your celebration. Check with your parents for the date, time, and address of the party. Make sure you are clear about all these details before you begin.
2. Decide on what your invitation will say. You may want to start with "*Habari gani!*" which means "What's

happening?" or "*Harambee!*" which means "Let's pull together!"
3. Practice writing your text on white paper. Make sure you fold the paper or cut it to the size you intend for the actual invitation.
4. Now you can begin. For a folded invitation, take your construction paper and fold in half.
5. On the outside you can write one of the greetings listed above or draw an African symbol.
6. Open the card and write the information about your event on the inside.
7. When you are finished, close the card again and glue cowrie shells or beads to your symbol.
8. If you use oak tag, cut it into a square or whatever shape you prefer.
9. Write your text in the center.
10. Turn the invitation over and draw your African symbol. If you like, you may glue cowrie shells or beads to it.

Craft: Make a Kinara

One way that the whole family can get involved in Kwanzaa is to make a kinara. You need to get a few supplies and clear a work space to begin. While you're working, remember to swap stories. Nearly everybody has an uncle who is great with his

hands. Parents share stories of Uncle Joe and what he made when they were young. You can have great fun sharing those stories, as you create your own right now.

What You Need

- Block of wood
- Pencil with eraser
- Ruler
- Drill (This is optional. You may have the wood cut for you.)
- Fine sandpaper
- Finishing wax
- Soft cloth
- Preglued velvet (optional)
- Fabric scissors
- Red, black, and green candles (either standard $^7/_8$-inch or $^{13}/_{16}$-inch diameter)

Getting Started

1. Go to a good lumberyard and buy a block of wood. A hardwood is the best choice: oak, cherry, mahogany, or ebony (if you can find it). These woods are more expensive, but they are well worth the extra cost, as they look beautiful when they are finished. You can use other types of wood as well.
2. Have the lumberyard cut your piece

of wood: 14$^1/_2$ inches long by 5 inches wide by 1$^3/_4$ inches thick. If you desire, you can make your block a little longer or thicker.

3. Marking lines with a pencil, divide the block of wood in half, making four quadrants. First divide the length in half and draw a line. Then divide the width in half and draw a line. This will give you the center point of your block of wood.

4. From your center point, measure 1$^3/_4$ inches in each direction, but only along the lengthwise line of your block. Draw a small mark. Measure another 1$^3/_4$ inches in both directions from the first set of marks, and draw a small mark. Then measure once again 1$^3/_4$ inches from the second set of marks. Draw a small line widthwise through each mark. You should now have seven cross marks on your block of wood.

5. These cross marks represent the centers of the seven holes you will drill or have drilled for the seven Kwanzaa candles.

6. Measure the candles you intend to use to see what size hole you need to drill. We recommend selecting standard-size candles whose diameters measure either $^7/_8$ of an inch or $^{13}/_{16}$ of an inch.

7. Get help in drilling the holes. If your parents are handy, ask them to help with this task. Or perhaps a shop teacher at school or someone at your lumberyard will do it for you using a drill press, so that the holes are straight. (This is very important.) Drill the holes to a depth of $^7/_8$ of an inch. Whatever you do, do not drill all the way through the block of wood.

8. Using fine sandpaper, carefully sand the block of wood all over. Take your time and make sure you sand off all pencil marks and any scratches in the wood. Sand your block until it is very smooth all over.

9. Wipe the block of wood clean with a soft, slightly damp cloth. Rub the block all over with a finishing wax, such as Finishing Wax by Minwax. You can buy a small can of wax at any good hardware store or at your lumberyard. Let the wood sit for a while, approximately 30 minutes. Then give your kinara a second coating.

10. Wait another 30 minutes and polish with a soft cloth.

11. Pull protective paper off the glued velvet. Carefully cover the bottom of your kinara with velvet, then trim carefully so the bottom is smooth and no edges stick out.

12. Add the candles and celebrate!

Craft: Make Your Mkeka Place Mat

The mkeka is the foundation of your Kwanzaa altar. It's the item on which all of your other elements sit. As the seat of honor, it needs to be spectacular. It's possible to actually weave a mat starting with pieces of fabric or cloth. You can also use a premade mat that you decorate.

What You Need
- Mat of some kind (woven, cloth, etc.)
- Ruler
- Pencil
- Hole puncher
- Colored raffia or yarn
- Scissors
- Paint
- Paintbrushes
- Cup for water

Getting Started
1. Measure 1 inch from each corner of your mat and mark with your pencil.
2. Punch a hole in the center of your pencil mark.
3. Measure the length of your mat between the two holes at either end and divide the space equally into 4 more points to place holes. Mark the space with your pencil and then use your hole puncher to create the holes. Count the number of holes you have made.

4. Select several threads of raffia, about 5, and measure 7 inches. Cut as many groupings of raffia as you have holes.

5. Thread the raffia through a hole and bring the ends together so that they are even. Tie the raffia tightly and knot it. Thread the raffia all around until you have threaded the entire mat. Now smooth out the raffia.

6. Using your paintbrush, paint your message onto your mat. Perhaps you want to write *Habari gani!* or What's happening! You may want to write Happy Kwanzaa. Or you can draw an African symbol in the center of your mkeka.

7. When your design is complete, let it sit for at least 30 minutes to allow the paint to dry. Then your mkeka is ready for your Kwanzaa festivities.

Popsicle Stick Picture Frame

Families take lots of pictures during Kwanzaa, so everybody needs picture frames. Make frames to share as zawadi.

What you Need
- Popsicle sticks
- A small candle and matches
- Glue
- White cardboard

Getting Started
1. Carefully burn the ends and the middle of 8 Popsicle sticks, using the candle. If children are too young to work with fire, an adult should do this part. All children should be supervised when handling fire.

2. Place the sticks on the cardboard: 2 on each side and 2 at the top and bottom. The sides should touch the ends of the top and bottom pair.

3. Trace around the sticks and in the middle area.

4. Cut the cardboard along the trace marks so that you have a rectangle with the center cut out.

5. Glue the 8 Popsicle sticks back in

place. Allow the glue to dry for about 10–15 minutes.

6. Turn the frame over and glue another 8 sticks on the frame along the sides and the top and bottom, exactly as you did on the front. The sticks on the back do not have to be burned.

7. Now, holding the frame in a vertical position, glue 4 sticks across the back of the picture opening. These sticks will be glued onto the side sticks. They are used to hold your picture in place.

As you plan your Kwanzaa celebrations, feel free to design events that are comfortable and allow your family to get the most out of it. Kwanzaa is a season of bounty, a perfect time for family members and loved ones to come together to share in the abundance of love and respect that you have for one another. Make the season count by paying attention to all of the details. Include everyone in your activities. Invite elders, neighbors, children, and teens to contribute to making these seven days memorable. Our heritage is powerful. When we invoke its power and meaning, as they are specific to our daily lives, we provide essential sustenance that will keep us strong over time.

chapter two

christmas

Honoring the Intention of the Holiday

PERHAPS THE MOST WIDELY CELEBRATED HOLIDAY OF ALL IS CHRISTMAS. Those of us who practice Christianity honor December 25, the date of Christ's birth, as one of the holiest days of the year, second only to Easter. For Christians, the holiday represents a time of reflection, a time to remember the great joy and hope that Christ brought to the world. People of many other religious traditions have come to celebrate the day as a secular holiday—a time for family to gather and share their love. Family members typically travel far and wide to be together during this season. Relatives make room for loved ones to stay in their homes, or arrange other lodging when the numbers swell beyond home capacity. Lots of preparation goes into decorating the home and preparing the most delicious meals. And, of course, there's a tremendous focus on gifts, especially for young ones.

Indeed, in the spirit of showering our love upon those we hold close to our hearts, we sometimes can go overboard when it comes to giving gifts. Over the years, as our families have become more prosperous, the abundance of gifts has expanded almost exponentially. Too many of us have become victims of our own big eyes, making purchases that extend our wallets beyond reason.

Like Kwanzaa, we can also approach Christmas in a different way. Rather than focusing on how much we can spend on gifts, let's look at this holiday with fresh eyes. Let's join with our family members, young and old, to come up with creative ways of honoring each other and the intention of this great holiday without upsetting the balance of our resources or our values. One way to start is by remembering why the holiday exists in the first place and creating a balanced understanding shared by everyone in the family.

The Three Wise Men

When Jesus was born in the manger in Bethlehem, he was born to parents of meager means in a community of people who lived a simple life. People did not have excess. Indeed, they got by happily, making do with the possessions that were theirs. Still, on great occasions people became resourceful in order to celebrate. Naturally, when word spread that the Son of God had been born, the news traveled across the land. And so, from far and wide people journeyed to pay homage to the holy birth, all the while following a bright star that suddenly appeared in the sky. Among them were the Three Wise Men. These men traveled to Bethlehem across miles of desert with prized gifts to offer Jesus. Many believe that the shepherds and others who came to visit Jesus in the stable brought their own humble gifts, too.

In the spirit of the Three Wise Men, we can offer special gifts to those we love. Our gifts need not require expense greater than we can afford. At the same time, they can represent the fullness of our love. As you consider what to give your loved ones, know your budget as a whole. Plan your list of loved ones whom you would like to offer a gift. Then think about each person individually and how you can honor your relationship. The cost of a gift really isn't what matters. Your

Remember the Star

Bringing stories to life for children helps them to understand the holiday and its impact on their lives. In my sister Stephanie's family, they make cookies every holiday. One year, Stephanie decided to make North Star Sugar Cookies with her children and our mother, Doris Cole, pictured above with Cole-Stephen, Stephanie's eldest son, as a way to teach her children about their heritage. Just as the Wise Men's star was the beacon of light that they followed as they charted their course to Bethlehem, the North Star guided thousands of our ancestors as they fled the shackles of slavery. While making cookies with her children, Stephanie and my mother were able to teach many lessons about African American history to Stephanie's eager children.

Begin your celebration of Christmas with reverence. Then, even in the midst of great fun and revelry with family and friends, all of you will remember that this is a time to honor each other, to practice being loving and kind. The children can light a candle in honor of the holiday, pledging their remembrance.

thoughtfulness and presentation are what count.

As you make your gift lists, do remember your spiritual home. Christmas is a holy time when we honor the life, lessons, and sacrifice of Jesus Christ. If you are Christian, by all means give a donation to your church for the work it offers. Should you practice a different religion, now's the time to acknowledge your own path.

The Spirit of Giving

Christmas is a time for giving. One of the best ways to give is of your creativity and time. Gifts offered from a spirit of generosity and love mean so much more than even the most expensive gift that comes out of obligation.

For some people, the Christmas season begins right after Thanksgiving and lasts through Kwanzaa and the New Year. As you and your family prepare for the festivities of the holiday season, take the time to think about ways which inspire your own spirit of generosity. Here are a few ideas:

Create a generosity circle: Sometimes it takes a spark of an idea for a group to get going. Everyone in your family, your friends, and neighbors—whoever is present—can gather in a circle to be together. Have each person talk about what generosity means to them. You can begin by saying, "I define generosity as . . ." or "I feel generous when . . ." and having them fill in the blanks. Give each person a few minutes to share whatever bubbles forth. Then with that incredible buildup of loving energy, tackle some projects that express your generosity tangibly. You may choose to host a fund-raiser for a retirement home in your neighborhood or send handmade cards and gifts to a family in West Africa. Or to bake cookies for all the neighbors or trim the Christmas tree for the elderly couple next door.

Make a family prayer: Develop a prayer together that includes each family member's wishes for the family and community. Use the theme of generosity as your starting point. Once you create your prayer, write it down and refer to it throughout the Christmas season. Paint it on holiday cards to give to loved ones. Reach out to those less fortunate in your own community and around the world. Let the spirit of generosity flow forth from your heart to your family, community, and neighbors.

Secret Santa

Large families have been doing this for years. Write each person's name on a slip of a paper, and put the names in a bag. Take turns drawing one name. You will be that person's "secret" Santa. You can do this even if some family members live far away. Just have someone who's responsible and can keep a secret to pick for you and tell you what name you've gotten. Set a price limit on the total amount of money that you can spend, anywhere from $5 to $100, as long as everyone in the family can comfortably manage the amount. You can think of this as a creativity incentive. The idea is for it to be easy for every single person. And that means that nobody can cheat and spend extra!

One married couple with limited disposable income one year decided to give themselves a $7 cap on what they could spend on gifts for each other that Christmas. It turned out that they had more fun that year than in a long time. Both of them really got into it. The husband got an assortment of goodies,

Being able to spend quality time across the generations is a true blessing. Those moments between grandparent and grandchild—like this one with George Lopez and Raisa Rhoden—are priceless. Somehow the stories swapped resonate within us many years later, always at the perfect moment.

including a beer stein from his favorite pub and a copy of his favorite childhood comic book. The wife got "yummy" bath products in all her favorite "flavors." Sticking to your limit makes it impossible to go out at the last minute and just pick up something. Instead, you really have to put your heart and mind into it.

When children are involved in family giving, it is possible to stick to a limit, but sometimes it's hard to stick to the one-name-from-a-bag philosophy. Often parents and loved ones find it hard to resist buying gifts for the little ones. To manage things, your family can decide in advance how to handle the children's gifts so that you still exercise discipline in giving and receiving. In this way, the children will learn to appreciate each one of their gifts because they will notice them all. Plus, they will learn to understand the value of a gift coming from the heart rather than simple abundance of items. Keep in mind when you do give extra to the children that you remember the teenagers.

Involve the children in the whole process, as soon as they are old enough. In this way, they will understand and embrace the family plan.

Prepare for Your Celebrations

Throughout the Christmas season, you can make each day special by inviting guests over and creating fun activities. As you prepare your home for guests, enlist your children in every detail.

Clean your home room by room. Give each child a specific task that is necessary and manageable. The older children can help the younger ones in this process of learning and preparing.

Decorate each room with special items, including those that the children have made. Be sure to encourage children to place their items in favorite locations around the house.

Make desserts in advance. See "Family Celebration Recipes" for ideas.

Decorate Inside and Out

Inspired to decorate the outside of your home? Go shopping for lights and decorations with your family and figure out fun scenes that you can design outdoors. Kids can help set up displays on the ground—anything from a crèche scene complete with manger, three wise men, and Jesus, to Santa, reindeer, and a sleigh. Children can hang lights on bushes and lower limbs of trees while parents can handle the climbing. If you live in an apartment, decorate your balcony and hallway with lights. Hang a wreath on your front door.

Make sure you have proper electrical cords to operate lights safely. Then each evening as the sun goes down, the children can be responsible for turning the outdoor display lights on.

Many families hang elaborate decorations and lights outside their homes. Get into the Christmas spirit by getting a group together to see the spectacular presentations in your city. You may want to visit each year to see how their decorations change. Take pictures of the homes you like the most. You may want to use the photos as holiday cards. It's easy to do. Take card stock that's a little larger than the photo when it's folded. Glue the photo onto the front of the card. Write your message on the inside, and you're set!

Host a Tree-trimming Party

Everybody loves a tree-trimming party. For your party, here's what you can do:

Opposite: Even in sunny Florida some families go all out creating fanciful scenes.

Top: The decorations on the tree adorn the centerpiece for your home during the holidays.

Above: When the ground is covered in a blanket of snow at Christmastime, holiday lights take on a magic of their own.

Little Things Count

Margaret Turner of Baltimore has been giving Christmas ornaments to her loved ones for years, whether they have a tree-trimming party or not. Her theme has been ornaments with the year engraved on them. Over the years people have built up collections of these precious relics, and with them great stories about Margaret. This has become such a great tradition that Margaret, a poet since childhood, has even written poetry that's inspired by the ornaments to share with her loved ones.

Select a tree: Decide if you want a real or artificial tree. Nothing beats the fresh evergreen smell of a live tree, but artificial trees can be reused year after year and you don't have to worry about pine needles falling all over the floor. Children love to go to a tree farm to pick their own tree. If you live in a city with a farm nearby, take the drive. You can show the children how trees grow and then teach them how to keep the tree alive in the stand with water when you bring it home.

Decide on a theme for your tree ornaments: To keep the season fresh, you may want to have a different theme each year so that your entire family can get involved in making and purchasing special ornaments. Or you may choose a color scheme to serve as a guide for everyone so each person has to bring an ornament in a particular color. Or you may want to use cultural ornaments that showcase your heritage. The Rawlings in North Carolina have been using angels every year to invoke the spirit of Jesus' love. My mother has two trees, one with traditional, multicolored ornaments on it, another with Afrocentric ornaments.

Share stories of past Christmases: While you decorate the tree you can share stories of years past. Perhaps someone went on a trip one year instead of joining the family event. What happened on that trip? A child can tell about the birth of his sister or brother in between Christmases.

Make it a potluck event: You can serve simple food at a tree-trimming party, particularly finger foods like cheese, fruit, nuts, and cookies that don't get in the way of your activities.

Create a Holiday Grab Bag

Bebe Granger really gets into the holiday spirit at Christmastime. Her husband, Al Cuyjet, says that she starts preparing for next Christmas right after she puts the decorations away at the beginning of the year. Bebe always was involved in arts and crafts, making holiday ornaments, creative cookies, and all sorts of gifts for her loved ones. Now that she has a young daughter, making the gifts is even more important. "The holiday is about doing things for people you love and care about," Bebe says. "A big part of that is for my daughter Alyssa to understand that the holiday is more about doing things for people you love and care about than giving or getting gifts. The important thing is to make it meaningful for the people you care about. I don't want her to get into the pattern of wanting more and more presents. I want her to understand that it's about more than that."

A few years ago, Bebe decided to create a holiday grab bag. In her bag, she put a handmade holiday ornament, and practical stocking stuffers such as a piece of fruit, miniature toiletries, and other affordable items she picked up here and there. Lots of people come over to visit throughout the holiday season, and this way she has something for everyone. Together with her daughter, she has painted snowmen, made pottery angels, and painted miniature birdhouses as tree ornaments to give away. What's most important for the grab bag is that everyone gets a special gift to remember the holiday.

Capture the Moment

Document the festivities to share year after year. Look around on Christmas Day. Everybody's all dressed up, looking special. Plus, more members of your family

Gather everyone together to document the joy of family this Christmas. Shown here are Christina and Larry Carr with their children, Ashley and Cameron.

are together than most any other time during the year. Take advantage of the gathering. Make sure somebody has a working camera with plenty of film—at least two rolls. Take pictures of young and old. Get the whole family together, plus individual shots of each nuclear family. You may want to get disposable cameras too, so that people can capture what's going on throughout the day.

When you get your film developed, have duplicates made and record the year on the back of each picture right away. Next year—or sooner—you can share the images you've taken with others. Make or buy picture frames, create photo albums for parents and grandparents. Get creative! See "Document Your Event" for more ideas.

Wrap Presents—It Can Be Fun

I will never forget Christmas Eve in my home in Baltimore. Invariably, there would be bags and boxes strewn all over the floor in the den, rolls of colorful wrapping paper, dispensers of clear tape, multiple pairs of dull scissors, lots of ribbon, and bags of multicolored bows. After all of the essentials were gathered—gifts, wrapping and tissue paper, and supplies—it would be time for the troops to set up shop. My mother, my sisters, and I would sit cross-legged on the floor and begin to wrap gifts.

Mommie made this activity so much fun for us, even as we were learning about the importance of presentation. We learned how to fold paper to fit neatly around even the most difficult box. We learned how to conserve tape and hide it so that the gift looked flawless when we were finished. When it came to ribbon, that's when we had extra fun. Using the edge of the scissors to shirr the ribbon and make curlicues was a favorite.

What we learned those many years ago was that every aspect of gift giving during the holiday can be special if we take care with each step we take. No matter how simple or elaborate the actual gift, each one deserved to be decorated with our special touches. You can do the same with your family. Make wrapping gifts a group experience, one where everyone learns how to honor the recipients by paying attention to each detail of presentation. To ensure that your wrapping gathering is a success, especially if you plan it for Christmas Eve, make sure that you have enough of the wrapping essentials as well as batteries for any battery-operated items that you may be giving on Christmas Day.

Go Caroling

My sisters and I used to go caroling every year with our mother when we were young. The moms in the neighborhood would have already set it up, inviting other families from the block to meet at a particular time to go caroling throughout the neighborhood. Everybody got dressed up in nice winter coats. All the girls wore mufflers back then with furry little hats.

One year, my younger sister Stephanie and I went to a retirement home to sing Christmas carols for the residents. As self-conscious young adults, we felt a little awkward in the beginning. It didn't help any that only one of us could really sing—Stephanie. I could get by. We both knew the carols, though. As we went from room to room offering our voices in song, one by one the residents looked up and acknowledged our presence. A few of them joined in. Others just sat back and enjoyed the moment. It was great fun for us. It didn't matter how well we could sing. Sharing our love through song with others was all we needed.

Attend a Christmas Eve Worship Service

Christian custom in many churches calls for late-evening or midnight services that are often exquisitely beautiful. By candlelight, some churches fill with songs in praise of the full meaning of Jesus' birth for our lives. This is a great occasion to bring young and older children, as it serves as a balance to the commercial side that is so predominant these days. Some churches run special programs for young children simultaneously with the main service. Involve your entire family in the festivities. On Christmas Eve, you can do something that your family will remember for years to come. Some ideas:

- Offer to create special gift cards for each member of the congregation. Buy precut card stock and Christmas- color paints (red, green, gold), and talk to your children about the message they would like to offer to all who attend church that night.

- Create a play for church including all the young people who are interested. Then find out if you can stage the play right after services before everybody goes home.

- Bake cookies or cupcakes for parishioners and hand them out as folks leave.

My mother, Doris Cole, and my niece Kori-Morgan wrap gifts together each year. The way a gift is presented is just as important as the gift itself. *Above*: The choir at Heritage United Church of Christ in Baltimore, Maryland.

To Organize a Caroling Outing

Form a group of singers. Ask your siblings, cousins, neighbors, and friends from school or church. Any number from two or three to ten will work.

Pick your favorite carols or hymns and agree on your repertoire. Then practice until you feel confident. That time you spend together practicing can be lots of fun too!

Take Turns Hosting Christmas Dinner

Some families go to the same homestead year after year. Wouldn't it be fun to travel once in a while? Chances are you have family members spread out across the country. Why not plan a trip this year? Everybody can still get together if you plan far enough in advance. Families whose parents live in different parts of the country will love this because they can take turns yearly and end up visiting everybody with regularity on special occasions. Those traveling from far away can still make their favorite dish, even if they have to do it at the host's home. Plus, this way your children get to see different parts of the country.

Sharing with Your Community

Generosity can be a pleasurable side effect of the holiday season. Instead of giving only to your own family, especially if they don't really need gifts, you can think more broadly.

Share Your Love at a Retirement Home

Christmas can be a lonely time for people who aren't near family. Sometimes people who live in retirement homes don't get to see their loved ones on Christmas Day or during the holiday season. You can give a few hours or a whole day at a nearby retirement home to help cheer people up. A fun, useful, and affordable gift you can bring is a goody bag filled with such daily essentials as soap, toothpaste, lotion, and powder. You can pick up these items in the dollar store or at your local grocery store. To make the package look nice, gather up the items that you will give each person. Wrap them in tissue paper and wrap again in holiday paper or put in small bags tied with ribbon. Small brown-paper lunch bags work fine when wrapped with a bright red ribbon. When you bring the gifts to the home, present each one individually. With a big smile on your face you can wish each person a happy holiday. The heart connection is what counts.

Plan Your Family Dinner

Christmas dinner can be lots of fun from the preparations all the way through. Do you have family traditions for the holidays? Think about what you do as a family and what your family did when you were growing up. You'll be amazed at how many creative ideas you and your family already have that can be loads of fun come Christmas dinner.

Set the table: A family tradition in my house was setting the table. For Christmas, we pulled out all the finery we had: tablecloths that belonged to my grandmother, dishes from my parents' wedding, silverware that was a combination of my parents' and grandparents' sets, serving dishes of all sizes and shapes, and glasses for water and wine.

Come Christmas Morning

I learned a funny lesson from my sister Susan many years ago. Before she comes out of her room on Christmas Day, she's dressed and ready to go. While my sister Stephanie and I used to clamor for gifts, figuring out who could get there first and later, just relaxing and being leisurely about formally starting our day, Susan was raring to go. Well, when we reviewed family photos a few years ago, wouldn't you know it? Susan is the one who stood out as looking clean, crisp, and ready to have her picture taken!

A word to the wise: when you get up on Christmas morning, get dressed early. You'd be surprised how early people start coming over to visit. To ensure that the pictures taken during the holidays reflect the true you that you want everybody to see, give yourelf a few extra minutes to get ready.

Above: From the preparations through the last dish being washed, Christmas Day is one to remember. Folks come together, some who see each other once a year. Children rekindle bonds of family and friendship. At my cousin Patricia Branch's Christmas dinner, everybody gets to catch up on each other's lives. *Opposite*: Caroling is a rewarding activity, especially for teens.

Preparing the table was a task that began days before Christmas. Each of us had a responsibility in the preparations, and with each task came a story from Mommie. You can do the same with your family, to keep your family lore alive as you also reinforce good table manners.

Select the tablecloth and napkins: Choose a family heirloom cloth that has a great story attached to it. Maybe you have your grandmother's linen cloth that's been passed down for generations. Or start a tradition by going with your children to purchase a tablecloth that you will use each year for special holiday meals.

Iron the linens: When supervised, older children can be great at ironing the table linens for Christmas dinner.

Clean the silver: If you have sterling silver flatware, water pitchers, serving bowls, or other items, you will probably have to clean them before use. Children can help with this task, under supervision. As you clean each item using silver polish and a soft cloth, tell the story of how you came to own the items. You'll be surprised at the stories that you recall. One family told us that while cleaning silver with their mother and grandmother, they learned that it was a tradition during their grandmother's time for people to purchase one silver utensil or place setting—depending upon how much you could afford to spend—per year to give to married couples. Over the years they would come to own a complete set of silverware.

Set up a children's table: You'd be amazed at the memories that you can recall from childhood activities with family. Many adults reminisce about feeling all grown up when they got to sit at their own table for Christmas dinner. For years, Pearl Cole Brackett, my father's sister, hosted Christmas dinner for our family. The older folk would come and sit around and talk, while the children had their own room and table. As they were getting all dressed up for the day, they got excited knowing that they would be guests of honor at a perfectly set miniature table with matching chairs. They felt special all day long, and so can your children.

Develop the menu: Invite the whole family to submit ideas for Christmas dinner. Especially since family members love to bring their special dishes, have everybody participate. Children can help to make family specialties that they help to serve at the meal.

Cook together: At each family home Christmas meal preparation is a fun and necessary activity. During the preparation remember to tell stories about Christmases past. The little ones can learn about what was done in the past, while older children can add their own memories to the mix.

Adopt a Family

Just as some people give money for other families to have a turkey dinner for the holiday, others actually "adopt" a family and spend time with them during the holidays. You can find families who are in need through your church, a shelter in your neighborhood, or your local newspaper. It's best to check with the administrators to see what family might be interested in having you be a part of their lives. Remember that as interested as you are in being of support to others, the family has to be willing and interested in receiving your generosity in order for it to bear fruit.

Select Your Music

When you're planning your caroling be sure you know the music that you want to sing. If you belong to a choir at school or at church, check in to see if there are any new songs you like or new arrangements that can make your caroling fresh. Here are some favorites from longtime carolers:

"O Come, All Ye Faithful"
"Joy to the World"
"The Little Drummer Boy"
"Silent Night"
"Jingle Bells"
"Away in a Manger"
"Hark! The Herald Angels Sing"
"Do You Hear What I Hear?"
"We Wish You a Merry Christmas"
"O Holy Night"

- You can sing with small portable instruments such as tambourines, a cappella, or accompanied by a tape or CD. Make sure you pack your musical supplies when you actually go caroling.
- Assign someone to be choreographer—whoever has the most natural gift with rhythm and dance—and practice singing your carols with your dance moves.
- Decide on your wardrobe. Will you wear costumes? Coordinate colors?
- Research local facilities that may welcome your caroling—your church's outreach affiliates, retirement homes, hospitals. Speak to the proper officials to set it up.
- Rehearse once or twice a week to get your routine together.
- Gather at the appointed time and go for it! Sing from your hearts, sharing your love with others.

My sister, Stephanie Hill, takes time during the holidays to make her specialty, Rum Cake à la Stephanie, with her daughter, Kori-Morgan.

Talk to your own family about how you might "adopt" another family this Christmas. The choices vary tremendously. Here are a few possibilities:

- Contact a social services organization in your city to see if they have names of families who would be interested in your kindness. Programs for mothers and children who are at risk are often a good place to start.
- Find out what the most needed items are for the family. Usually clothing, food, and toys are at the top of the list.
- Purchase a Christmas tree for them along with a variety of ornaments, lights, and garlands.
- Make or purchase gifts for each member of the family, especially the children.
- Make or purchase Christmas stockings for each member of the family.
- Go to a dollar store with your family to pick out fun and practical items to stuff stockings and make an abundant holiday celebration for them.
- Make a holiday card that everyone in your family signs. Include good wishes for the happiness and prosperity of the family you've adopted.
- Be sure that all of your offerings to the family come from your heart.

Teen Time: Stage a Christmas Play

Wouldn't it be great fun for the whole family to get involved in a creative project for Christmas? Teens can organize it. Cousins, brothers and sisters, parents, aunts and uncles, and friends can join the fun. Somebody who's creative can write a new version of the story of Jesus that may even include your family and how His lessons have affected your lives.

Find a time when everybody's free, preferably not Christmas Day, when there are already lots of activities planned. Find a location—such as a family basement or living room—where you have enough room to stage your play. Design costumes that illustrate the characters in your play. Make a schedule to practice. Send out handwritten invitations to all of your guests. Then, when you perform your play, have a blast. Everyone will be so happy to see your creativity.

Make a Memorabilia Mantel

Christina and Larry Carr and their two children, Cameron and Ashley, remember their family members during the holidays by creating a mantel dedicated to them. They frame pictures of everyone who's living as well as those who have passed on. Then they dedicate one mantel over a fireplace to family portraits. Each year they take time out to look at the portraits together and tell stories of each person. Some stories are funny, others serious.

You can do this too: Ask family members if they have old photos of relatives who are often in your thoughts but whose faces you don't quite remember. Place them on your memorabilia mantel or on a table devoted to your loved ones. Be sure to include your brothers and sisters as well as your parents on this table too. Everybody who's part of the family can be represented, so that as you share stories about each person, the lineage continues right up to the present.

Christmas Dinner

Coconut Chips

Grandma T's Fresh Fruit Cup

Old-Fashioned Apple Chicken Salad

Little Hands Mixed Salad

Special Soy Roast Chicken

Gum-Gum's Corn Pudding

Celebration Spinach

Garlic Mashed Potatoes

North Star Sugar Cookies

Rum Cake à la Stephanie

Iced Tea Punch

There may be no better feeling than that of accomplishing a creative task. With a few key items, you can draw upon your own creative resources and make the perfect gift for someone you love. Before starting, think about the recipient and what the person really likes. Let that inspiration guide you.

Let Creativity Reign!

As we did for Kwanzaa, we can spend quality time together with family members in the days and weeks ahead of Christmas by making presents together. In this way, we demonstrate that each of the steps leading up to giving the gift is important. Indeed, the effort and love put in are far more important than the cost of the item. Make time to create gifts together! Some of the best memories are born in the process.

Make Holiday Gifts

Devote weekends and evenings before Christmas to making special gifts for your loved ones.

Craft: Design Decorative Boxes

Making decorative boxes can be lots of fun, and they are fantastic gifts, especially for girls. You can use cardboard boxes that you paint, wooden boxes that you put together and paint, or plastic boxes with ready-made tops that you decorate. Here's how to make a seashell masterpiece:

What You Need:

- Small plastic box with top (available at art-supply and craft stores)
- Glue gun with extra glue sticks
- Bag of seashells (available at art-supply and craft stores, or from your own gatherings at the beach)
- Hard, flat surface to work on
- Newspaper to protect the floor

Getting Started:

1. Sort seashells according to size and shape.
2. Plug in glue gun and insert glue stick. (Glue warms quickly.)
3. Look at your box and plan a design with your shells that will artfully cover your box. You may want to use a large shell on top that will serve as a handle to use when pulling the top off.
4. Once you have a clear idea of your design plans, select your beginning point and apply glue. Immediately adhere a shell to the hot glue and hold it in place for a few seconds.
5. Move onto the next spot. Apply glue and adhere a shell.
6. Continue until you have completed your design.

Note: We bought our shells in a bag that was also filled with fragrant potpourri. Once the box was decorated, we filled it with the dried colorful flowers to make an extra-special gift.

Craft: Create Pipe-cleaner Ornaments

Bebe Granger is chock-full of creative ideas. Among them is the creation of pipe-cleaner ornaments that very young children can help make.

What You Need:

- Colorful pipe cleaners
- Plastic beads in different colors and shapes
- Candy canes
- Red and white string

Getting Started:

1. Bend pipe cleaners into interesting shapes such as circles, triangles, or stick figures.
2. Thread beads onto pipe cleaners, bending tips afterward to hold in place.
3. Either wrap pipe cleaner around candy cane to secure it or tie ribbon around cane tight enough that it will stay in place.
4. Using candy cane as hook or string, hang ornament on tree.

Craft: Embellish Glass Ornaments

Another easy-to-follow activity is embellishing ornaments that you already have or that you purchase.

What You Need:

- An assortment of colorful glass ornaments (clear, red, gold, green, silver, whatever you like)

- Small pinecones, seashells, or beads, pearls that come by the yard
- Decorative ribbon
- Glue gun

Getting Started:

1. Place ornament in front of you and select location for ornamentation.
2. Select item to place on ornament—pinecone, seashell, etc.
3. Apply glue to ornament in the selected spot.
4. Gently attach the item onto the spot and hold it for a few seconds.
5. Tie a ribbon in a bow and glue it to the top of the ornament, right in front of the hook that goes on the tree.
6. Then you are ready hang the "new" ornament.

Craft: Make Decorative Vines

Children will delight when decorating vines and ivy to place around the house.

What You Need:

- 3-inch grapevine leaf sections (as many as you like)
- Ribbons or bows
- Dried flowers
- Candy canes
- Glue gun

Getting Started:

1. Open up vine so that it's relatively flat.
2. Make bows out of ribbons.
3. Using glue gun, affix ribbons in strategic locations on vines leaving room for other items.
4. In between ribbons, affix clusters of dried flowers and candy canes or other items you like.
5. When finished, place or hang vines around your home.

Craft: Design Personalized Picture Frames

The sky is the limit for your creativity when you start with an unfinished picture frame. Let your imagination run free. Painting different designs and/or your name with your paintbrush is just one option. Buttons, bottle caps, and other objects can be glued to the frame to show how creative you can be.

What You Need:

- Unfinished picture frame (available at art-supply store)
- Paint
- Paintbrushes
- Paper cups for water
- Water
- Glue
- Fabric
- Buttons, bottle tops, and other found objects

Getting Started:

1. Think about the person you want to give a picture frame. What is the person's style? Look at your materials to see how you can incorporate them into a design that reflects the person.
2. You have several options. You can either paint a design on your picture frame or affix fabric to the frame, giving it the feeling of interior design, or you can glue buttons, bottle tops, seashells, or other objects onto the frame.
3. Clean up the edges of the frame once you have created your design.
4. Be sure to give the frame plenty of time to dry before you stand it up, at least 20 minutes.
5. Using paint, sign your name on the back of the frame.

Craft: Design a T-Shirt

Be creative this Christmas. You don't have to get your dad a tie this year! Show him how much you love him by designing a T-shirt just for him. It's easy and fun to do.

What You Need:

- Plain white cotton T-shirt in his size. If you aren't sure, ask your mom or buy a size L or XL. (It's better to be too big than too small.)
- Masking tape
- Different colors of puff paint—a type of paint that comes in a spray can.
- Hard, flat surface.
- A few pieces of plain white paper for practicing

Getting Started:

1. Set up your work space. Puff paint is pretty easy to use and it doesn't spill much. To be safe, though, put newspaper on the floor to catch any excess paint.
2. Think about the person you are making the shirt for. What do you love about him or her the most? Can you put your feelings in words or in an illustration?
3. When you have a sense of what you want to do, go to your white paper. Tape the paper to your flat surface so that it won't shift when you're working on it.

4. Practice writing letters with the puff paint or making your drawing. Notice how you can control the thickness of the paint and, in turn, the dimension of your design. Puff paint is great because it can bring your ideas to life in fun ways that flat paint cannot.

5. Once you feel comfortable with your idea, move to your T-shirt. Place your master—your design on paper—next to you for reference.

6. Tape your T-shirt to the flat surface. Make sure you put tape on the neck, the sleeves, the sides, and the bottom of the shirt. Don't pull the T-shirt too hard, just enough to make the fabric flat and even.

7. Now, begin painting. Watch your masterpiece emerge. Your dad will be so proud!

Craft: Make Holiday Cards

Every year when I was a little girl, my Aunt Hattie used to invite me over to her house to help her write out Christmas cards. She was about 80 years old then. Even though she had great intentions, her eyesight just didn't allow her to manage writing out all those cards to the people she wanted to remember for the holidays. So, it became my job. I got to see all the different kinds of cards that people can send during the holidays. And, one time, I actually made some cards that Aunt Hattie could send along with the ones she had already purchased. She loved my cards. You can make holiday cards too. Your family will be so happy to see your personal creations that you have made just for them.

What You Need:

- Precut blank 5-inch by 8-inch cards, either postcard format or folded (You can get these at an art-supply store.)
- White paper
- Assorted colors of water-based paint and/or puff paint
- Colored markers (optional)
- Paintbrushes
- Palette

- Glitter
- Glue
- Hard, flat surface

Getting Started

1. Check your list to see who will receive a handmade holiday card. Do you want to make one for everybody? For your parents and godparents? Count how many you need to make and keep track as you go along.

2. What message do you want to send? What will your card say? What will it look like? Do you have a favorite holiday scene you want to draw? A line from a poem you love? A verse from Scripture you want to send to everyone?

3. Practice painting your message on white paper.

4. If you have chosen a folded card and you want to include a message on the inside, write that message with your marker now.

5. When you're ready, paint the outside of your card. Let it dry for at least 30 minutes.

When school is out, and the family is together, the moment is ripe for being together. Remember to welcome each person who arrives to your home with a smile and an open heart. Extend your love to everyone. Your joy is contagious. At the same time, be sure to give each other space. Sometimes you just need to be alone to think and reflect. Parents can support their children during this time by giving them the tools for creative expression. In this way, they may be inspired to draw upon their own inner resources rather than being entertained by the television or video games. Make the Christmas season count. Your loved ones are worth it.

chapter three

naming ceremonies

Capturing the Essence of Who We Are

THE IMPORTANCE OF A NAME CANNOT BE UNDERESTIMATED. OUR NAME accompanies us throughout our lives. Indeed, sometimes our names make an impression on someone before we do.

As in many cultures throughout the world, our ancestors understood the importance of naming loved ones and regarded it as a sacred activity. In traditional African communities—both in generations past and today—what children are named takes on huge spiritual and social significance. The elders of a village understand that whatever a child is called from the first day will affect the rest of his or her life. The name given to this new life must have meaning. The name must serve as a foundation from which this person can be supported and guided each and every day. Carefully chosen, inspiring names can even reveal to children their destiny.

Think about that for a moment. Embodied in our names is our destiny. When we give that serious thought, it makes perfect sense that we take time to give our children names that will support and guide them in their lives. It is from this awesome responsibility that our naming ceremonies come.

Malidoma Somé, a writer and commentator on life in his small village in Burkina Faso, West Africa, talked in great detail about the importance of the naming ceremony in his book, *Of Water and the Spirit* (Penguin, 1995). Somé described the process as a spiritual one that requires great sensitivity on the part of the one discovering the name, because for the rest of the person's life he or she will be finding ways to fulfill the destiny inherent in the name. In Somé's culture, it is understood that even when individuals don't consciously choose to live up to the direction given by their name that their spirit guides them to do so. There is power in a name.

Naming Newborns

Great contemplation goes into selecting a name when you follow African principles. Commonly, the spiritual leader of the community is charged with divining the name—or conducting a spiritual ritual in which he or she asks the Creator to reveal the role of this human being in the form of a name.

Options abound for what to name your children. Key in the naming process is to select a name that has great meaning to your family and the new life that will assume the name. Find out all that you can about the name you are considering. This is a great activity for siblings to join. Children of all ages can talk with parents about the new baby and the possibilities of what to call him or her.

Families can research African names that will remind their children of their heritage and also inspire them as they live their lives. If you are looking for an African name, you may want to research names from one of the numerous African cultures, from which our people originated. There are some great books out now that list African names and their meanings, which can guide your search.

How can you decide on what to name your loved ones? It really depends upon what approach makes you comfortable. Your spiritual beliefs and how you go

Opposite: Rev. Calvin O. Butts blesses the life of Cameron Fane.

Above: The sand that Cameron's grandmother, Lana Turner, collected and offered ceremonially to honor this child's birth.

Below: Music and memories can make lasting impressions when you gather to welcome a newborn into the world.

about researching your name will determine how you secure it. In traditional West African communities, for example, people often reach out to oracles for guidance. The oracle essentially is a tool for people to use in order to communicate with God and the ancestors. Oracles come in many forms, such as cards, coins, bones, and other items, depending upon the culture. Of course, you would need someone who knows oracles to engage one on your behalf.

If you aren't involved in a spiritual community that uses oracles, don't worry. It's not necessary to work with an oracle. Many parents tell of learning their children's names in dreams. You'd be surprised at how often we receive such messages. The question is whether we pay attention or not. In the case of a dream, it serves as a revelation to the parents from God and the ancestors.

In other situations, parents gather to talk about their family members, those ancestors who have passed and whose memories they want to keep alive. They contemplate their ancestors and recall their personalities, drawing upon those family members whose lives exemplify honor, integrity, and possibility. Sometimes it becomes clear that the new baby has characteristics of a loved one who has passed, and so parents give the child that person's name to carry on.

The name can be of any origin that appeals to you. The reason that so many people are named Junior is because they are named in honor of their parents who may, in turn, have been named for their parents. It can be wonderful to be part of a family legacy that can be traced back for generations. When I was named, my parents drew upon both families for guidance. My father was named Harry Cole, so, in a way, though I am a middle child, I became "Junior," since there weren't any boys in my family. Also, on my mother's side, my great-great-grandmother was named "Harriette Ann," just like me. It turns out that this Harriette Ann was a strong woman who had bought her own freedom from slavery, as well as the freedom of her husband and children. When I learned about both sides of my name—my daddy, a powerful man of great integrity who achieved many firsts in his legal career, and my great-great-grandmother, who was a brave woman—I realized that I had a great legacy to uphold.

Similarly, legacy figured into the naming inspiration for John and Victoria Pinderhughes when their two daughters were born. Sienna, the firstborn, was named after the eponymous brown color. The sound of the word and the beauty of the color inspired them. When it came to their second child, John wanted to name her in honor of his father. He wanted to name her "Johnnai." But Mommy and Daddy didn't agree on that name or spelling. When they found the name Ghenet, they knew they were onto something. Ghenet is an Ethiopian name meaning "Heavenly Paradise." What they ended up being able to do was to honor John's father and their African heritage thanks to their efforts to find the name that rang true for them.

As with their family, once you know the name you want to use—generally within the first seven days of the infant's life—preparations begin for a great celebration that welcomes this new life into the world.

A Grandmother's Love Story

When Lana Turner learned that her son and his partner were expecting a baby, she immediately began planning a special celebration to honor the child's birth. Upon the birth of the baby boy, Cameron, Lana went all out to celebrate the entrance of this future man into the world. Her intention was to create a foundation that would stand the test of time, a grand celebration that would demonstrate to Cameron for years to come just how much he was loved from his first days of life. Here's what she did:

The Sacred Ceremony

Lana is a longtime member of Abyssinian Baptist Church in Harlem, New York. She arranged to have Cameron and his parents, Michael Fane and Valecia Ambrose, included in the ceremonial blessing of babies that Rev. Calvin O. Butts holds each month. Before the entire congregation, Rev. Butts held the baby Cameron up, asking for God's blessings and guidance as well as the love of all assembled.

A Tribute to Life

That afternoon about 200 family members and friends gathered at a beautiful old mansion for a joyous celebration. A ten-year-old played the baby grand piano. Children read poetry, played drums, and otherwise offered their talents in honor of Cameron. Cameron's parents testified on his behalf, articulating their love and intentions for him, as did his grandparents. His mother explained that the baby was given this name because it called out to her and his father as they were considering names. Cameron is originally a Scottish surname probably meaning "crooked nose" or "crooked hill" in Gaelic. Its literal meaning had minimal significance to Cameron's parents, but the music of the name resounded for them both. Its meaning worked too, in that Valecia said she didn't want her son to feel the pressure to be perfect, just to be the best he could be.

The entire experience was videotaped so that in years to come Cameron will be able to reflect on the powerful and abundant love that welcomed him into the world.

A Foot in the Past

A ritual was born out of this event. Lana had brought vials of sand that she and her family have collected from all parts of the world—from Namibia, Orchard Beach, New York; Jupiter, Florida; and Phoenix, Arizona. Rev. Butts prayed for Cameron's future as he reminded the child and all of us gathered of the importance of knowing the past—as he placed Cameron's feet in the sand, thereby leaving his footprint in that special place.

The Lullaby

To round out a full event, Lana offered one more special treat. She commissioned the musical director for the Dance Theatre of Harlem to compose a lullaby specifically for Cameron. At the event, Joseph E. Fields performed it for all of us.

Be Inspired by Your Surroundings

Just as Lana Turner included her spiritual home and elements of her family's heritage in her grandson's celebration, you can draw upon your own experiences and surroundings to craft your celebration. Think about what's important to your family, including sacred songs and prayers, family rituals, ancestral homestead, clothing and textiles, and more. You can design a naming ceremony that's perfect for your tastes and interests.

Twelve Steps to Your Naming Ceremony

We talked to a number of families and spiritual leaders about creating a naming

Naming Ceremony Program

Welcome: Parents or Grandparents of Newborn.

Libation: Pouring of water into a wooden bowl or on the ground if you're outside, as acknowledgment of those in your families who have passed.

Blessing: Officiate of event.

Invocation of Ancestors: Prayer including drumming that is traditionally used to invite ancestors to join festivities.

Poetry Recitation: A young person can read a poem about the newborn or another poem that celebrates life.

Words of Wisdom: Time for the family elder to speak about the family lineage.

Tasting Ceremony: Yoruba ritual acknowledging stages of life.

Calling the Name: Officiate followed by parents and all gathered repeat the child's name and its meaning, as a chant.

Feast and Blessing: Host can invite everyone to eat at this time, starting with a blessing for the future of the child and the family.

Closing Prayer: Host or officiate to end the afternoon with a prayer that sends people off with blessings.

Above right: Invite children to offer their talents at your child's naming ceremony. Here, Parker McAllister plays the piano at Cameron's naming ceremony.

ceremony. What we learned is that there are no hard-and-fast rules. This is mainly because we are adopting an African ritual and traditionally these rituals are passed down from generation to generation without being written down in manuals. Plus, in each community the rules change a bit. What's most important is for your intention to be clear. When the event is for an infant, of course, the parents and relatives have to organize all the details. When the event is for a teenager or an adult who is choosing to change a name, by all means that person should be involved in every detail.

1. **Do your research.** Find out what's important to you as a family and a community. What cultural references are important for you to incorporate into your daily life? By reading about African and African American heritage you may discover what rings true in your heart as to how to proceed.

2. **Learn your own family history.** Don't overlook who you are and how important your family is to your life today. Remember those who have passed on whose memories you still keep alive.

3. **Pray about it.** To name a human being is a sacred action. Treat it as such by praying about it—alone and with your family. In your prayer you may ask God what the child's destiny will be. Listen to your heart as you pray. Great inner wisdom may appear. Be sure to give every family member ample space to talk about what came up in their prayers. So often the least likely person to offer insight is ready with the perfect information.

4. **Pay attention to your intuition.** If you recall loved ones during this period of contemplation, notice their presence. In African heritage, we learn that the ancestors do present themselves to us when we need them. Perhaps a grandparent, uncle, or trusted family friend whose memory you have invoked carries the same type of spirit as your child.

5. **Make an invitation list.** Who are the special people in your life who will be happy to celebrate this occasion with you? All family members can participate in creating the list, adding family and friends as well as close neighbors. Be sure not to tell anyone about the event, though, until you have finalized your list. Sometimes the first list we come up with is very long and needs to be edited to accommodate the space where you will have the event as well as your budget.

6. **Set the date.** For spiritual purposes you may want to have the ceremony seven days after the child's birth. Or you may want to select a date that is convenient for everyone. In that case, check with key folks on your list to select the best possible date—preferably on a weekend afternoon when the child will be awake and family members have time to spend together.

7. **Plan the naming ceremony activities.** This includes who will speak, what role everyone will play, what amount of time the entire event will take, etc.

8. **Create your menu.** Consult with the great cooks in your family for ideas. Make it a real family affair by inviting others to make specific dishes. Just like any other great family gathering, this one will require a

Rev. Butts places Cameron's feet in the mixture of sand as grandmother Lana Turner explains the significance of the sand to all gathered.

memorable feast. Be sure to include lots of healthy goodies for the children and lots of easy-to-reach snacks for everyone.

9. **Plan your decorations.** Include children by inviting them to come up with their own ideas that they can execute in advance of the big day. (Remember that your children are just as excited as you are to welcome the new member of the family into the fold.) You can select a color scheme—and banners can be made with the newborn's name on them. One family hosted their naming ceremony during Kwanzaa, so the decor was already set—there would be a kinara and the feast of the karamu. Everyone was already in the spirit of family celebration, so it worked out perfectly.

10. **Make your invitation.** And be sure to include a dress code. Some families invite guests to wear African-inspired attire. Others request Sunday best. How we present ourselves for such a high occasion is important. Let everyone know so that you create a really festive occasion.

11. **Give young people specific responsibilities.** Too often young people feel left out because they don't have anything to do. Have a family meeting to discuss options for everyone's involvement. Some ideas include: setting the table, creating decorations for the room, helping to prepare food, greeting guests as they attend (with a big smile on their faces!), making sure the background music on the CD player is appropriate, as well as turning it off during the ceremony.

12. **Give elders special roles.** Think ahead about how the elders in your family can be honored at this occasion. You may invite the most elder female and/or male to say a few words about the child being named. Be sure to have proper seating for them so that they are comfortable. Assign a teenager to look out for them as the flurry of festivities gets underway.

- **Words of Wisdom:** Time for the family elder to speak about the family lineage
- **Tasting Ceremony:** Yoruba ritual acknowledging the stages of life
- **Calling the Name:** Officiate followed by parents and all gathered repeat the child's name and its meaning, as a chant
- **Feast and Blessing:** Host can invite everyone to eat at this time, starting with a blessing for the future of the child and the family
- **Closing Prayer:** Host or officiate to end the afternoon with a prayer that sends people off with blessings

An African Tale

Although many urban African families have become very Westernized, that doesn't mean that they don't hold onto tradition. Agunda Okeyo, a young woman from Zaire who has spent half of her life in Africa and half in the United States, says that her family takes great pride in passing names on from ancestors to newborns. She says, "The naming of a child is a sacred action, especially in cases where the child is named in honor of someone because from that name they derive their inner strength and honor." In her case, her mother had a dream in which her aunt Agunda presented herself just before little Agunda was born.

(Continued on page 68.)

Blessing the food and the gathering is an integral part of our celebrations. Here, Michael Fane and Valecia Ambrose join their parents and their son's godparents in blessing this naming ceremony meal for Cameron.

Choosing African Names

Some families choose African names for their children to serve as an immediate connection to their African heritage.

To get you started on your search for African names and their meanings, review this chart. Then research names. Look online as well as in books specifically devoted to African culture for ideas. There are many additional names that you can consider.

Girls' Names	Origin	Meaning
Adenike (ah-deh-NEE-kay)	Yoruba	Crown is loving and affectionate
Azalee (ah-zah-LEE)	Bini	Singer
Aziza (ah-ZEE-zah)	Kiswahili	Gorgeous, precious
Bahati (bah-HAH-tee)	Kiswahili	She who has fortunes for us all
Becca (BEH-cah)	Bogangi	Prophet
Bolade (BOH-lah-deh)	Yoruba	Honor arrives
Dene (DEH-neh)	Mande	Water lily
Hazika (ha-ZEE-kah)	Hausa	Intelligent one
Kali (KAH-lee)	Senufo	Energetic
Lerato (leh-RAH-toh)	Tswana	Love
Njemile (n-jeh-MEE-leh)	Kiswahili	Upstanding
Rashida (rah-SHEE-dah)	Kiswahili	Righteous
Serwa (sair-WAH)	Ewe	Noble woman
Subira (soo-BEE-rah)	Kiswahili	The reward of patience
Yakini (YAH-kee-nee)	Kiswahili	Truth
Zakiya (zah-KEE-yah)	Kiswahili	Intelligent

Boys' Names	Origin	Meaning
Abdullah (ab-DU-luh)	Arabic	Servant of God
Adnan (ahd-NAN)	Kiswahili	Good fortune
Akua (a-KOO-ah)	Faute	Sweet messenger
Ande (ahn-DEH)	Tigrinya people of Eritrea	Stable and unwavering, like a pillar
Chike (CHEE-keh)	Ibo	The power of God
Chipego (chee-PAY-goh)	Tonga people of Zambia	He whose presence is a gift among us
Dakarai (dah-kah-RAH-ee)	Shona	Joy
Ehioze (eh-HEE-oh-ZAY)	Benin	Above the envy of others
Jomo (JOH-moh)	Kikuyu people of Kenya	Burning spear
Ligongo (lee-GOHN-goh)	Malawi	What manner of man is this?
Thabiti (thah-BEE-tee)	Muera	A true man

MEDITERRANEAN SEA

Northern Africa

Ancient Egypt and Nubia

Sahel and Savanna

Western Africa

Eastern Africa

Guinea Coast

Central Africa

ATLANTIC OCEAN

Southern Africa

- Ancient Egypt + Nubia
- Eastern Africa
- Southern Africa
- Central Africa
- Western Africa + the Guinea Coast
- Sahel and Savanna
- Northern Africa

INDIAN OCEAN

Great Zimbabwe Ruins

Similarly, Agunda remembers the story of her Uncle Olando. He was blessed with the name of her grandfather Hosea Pala's close friend David Olando. Hosea and David met in grammar school and became fast friends. Their friendship took them through their higher education, marriage, and family and persisted even when their lives took them far from each other. One fateful day, Hosea was informed that his old friend had suddenly died. According to Agunda, her distraught grandfather jumped on his bike and peddled the forty miles to David's house. By the time the exhausted and emotionally stricken Hosea arrived, David had been buried. Hosea fell off his bike onto the warm country grass and cried hysterically for the confidant he could no longer see. Hosea went to the grave to bid his friend farewell, though the ache in his heart persisted.

Soon after, his wife, Agnes Bolo, was due to have another child. Hosea took her to the nearest hospital as a precaution, and he went back home to tend to the other children. The morning after Agnes gave birth, Hosea was awakened by a light tapping on his shoulder. He looked up slowly to find a grinning David Olando standing over him. "Wake up now, Hosea. Agnes has given birth to a son," David said. "Name him Olando for me." When Hosea arrived at the hospital, he was greeted by Agnes and a new baby boy, whom he immediately named Olando.

Be Mindful

African names are quite popular right now, as are names that only sound African. Names of famous TV and movie stars, fashion designers, and other celebrities also top the lists today of popular names for children. Don't fall into that shallow trap. You can empower your children and yourself by selecting a name with a known meaning. In this way, over the years you can go back again and again to the purpose of that person's life. The barometer for selecting a name needs to be something significant that will support the child throughout his or her life.

Changing Your Name

In addition to naming newborns, some people change their names at different points in their lives. The reasons vary. Of course, many women change their surnames when they marry, adding their husband's name to theirs. Sometimes people change their names for spiritual reasons. Other times it's for cultural reasons. During the 1960s and 1970s many African Americans adopted Islamic and African names that showed their connection to their African heritage. In so doing, they also commonly took time to learn about the African people among whom their name originated and took great pride in cultivating characteristics that celebrated their way of living.

Carrying on that tradition, many individual families adopt African names for their children and for themselves. Sometimes the naming activity happens after birth, at the point of puberty or whenever one is inspired to tap into a different aspect of their heritage. Rites of Passage groups have begun to gain momentum throughout the country as families seek out ways to support the adoption of a new name. One such group in Atlanta has organized an effective way of working with young people to align them with their heritage. Known as Nzinga for women and Ndugu for men, this organization was founded by Dr. Daniel Black, a brother who's affectionately known as Baba Omotosho. The first group, or "family" to experience this process was a group of males called the Adebayos.

When baby Sahar received her name, her parents, Maya and Nkozi, her grandparents, godparents, and other family members made the event a Kwanzaa celebration.

As a part of their "crossing" in 1993, they were each given new names of African origin. After they crossed, subsequent families (composed of both males and females) who crossed similarly participated in a naming ceremony.

During one subsequent ceremony, males and females of a single "family" gathered in a candlelit room facing a council of elders. One at a time, each initiate was called to stand alone among the elders while the other initiates called out his or her characteristics and traits. This continued for several moments while the council members gathered to review their resources—African naming guides— as well as to discuss and arrive at an appropriate name. Once the name was chosen, it was repeated, along with its meaning, for everyone to hear. The newly named then repeated his or her new moniker and walked to one side of the room. After each initiate was named, everyone again repeated his or her new name and the ceremony ended in prayer.

During this ceremony and others like it, the meanings of the names given are meant to both reflect one's spirit and highlight significant life lessons. As the list on page 66 indicates, the names are drawn from an array of African nations and peoples. Review this list to see if any name stands out for you. What's most important when you name a child or yourself is that you know the meaning and origin of the name. It is in this way that you can be empowered by the name that is invoked every time you enter a room.

If You Want to Change Your Name and You Are a Minor

If you want to change you name and you are a minor, talk to your parents about your wishes. Do your research so that you can present them with a name and a reason for wanting to add or change the name you already have. Sometimes people add names that loved ones call them, even though they don't change their names legally. It works the way nicknames do, the only difference being your chosen name can hold great power because it will have been selected with the utmost love and respect. There are many options that make it possible for you to celebrate yourself through your name. Find the one that works best for you.

The Tastes of Life

There's a common activity in Yoruba tradition that you might want to have for your naming ceremony—a tasting of the different aspects of life. The family pictured on page 69—Maya, Nkozi, and their daughter Sahar—followed Aunt Terri's lead. Terri Wisdom is active in her spiritual community and felt clear about how to honor the newborn. She organized the tasting ceremony that symbolized the stages of life that everyone goes through. This ceremony is designed to show that through fortitude, faith, and understanding about the road ahead the family can be triumphant. What you need to replicate this ceremony are five small bowls and the following items: honey, salt, pepper or spices, lemon, and water.

These items are used in the following ways:

1. Once everyone is gathered, with the mother and father and newborn at the center of the group, the celebrant of the naming ceremony can pour a libation (plain water) as an offering to the ancestors. If you are indoors, you can pour the libation into a wooden bowl. Otherwise, you can pour the water directly onto the ground.

2. Next, a family prayer can be offered. You may want to hold hands during the prayer. Make sure that the one offering the prayer speaks clearly and loudly enough for all gathered to hear.

3. Following the prayer, the celebrant will offer each of the four elements to the parents and child. The honey represents the sweetness of life. Salt stands for life's flavor. Pepper or spices represent the spiciness or heat of life. Lemon stands for the bitterness life can bring. Water represents neutrality.

4. After the parents taste the elements, everyone else gathered tastes each item.

Add Special Touches

At Sahar's naming ceremony all kinds of special things happened. Because it was held during Kwanzaa, the kinara was there to light the way to the strengthening of the African American community. Sahar's uncle, Wayne Duncan, who is a practicing Native American priest, also brought specific blessings. He offered a prayer to Sahar, her parents, and the entire family and he also shared a peace pipe with everyone present. In this way, he explained that Sahar would be blessed in every tradition that touches her life, thereby supporting her even further in her pursuit of a great life.

A spontaneous activity occurred at Sahar's ceremony that everyone will remember. Her cousin Hannibal, then four years old, perched himself on a chair in front of a big West African drum and began drumming. Turns out, Hannibal is quite an accomplished drummer, and he led the group in a joyous interlude for about half an hour.

Honor Your Name

Whatever you are named, know what it means and take the time to acknowledge who it says that you are. If you find that you want to change your name, that's fine too. It's never too late to adopt a new name. Although honoring the name your family gave you counts for a lot, if you find that your path leads you in another direction, go for it. What's most important is that you claim the full meaning of your name. Every time someone speaks your name, your entire being is invoked. Let that count for something. You can honor that meaning by learning the history of your name and contemplating what it means as your signature.

Your Feast

The meal for your naming ceremony can be a grand feast with all kinds of good food. Make sure you have lots to drink and plenty of snacks, so that people can nibble during the festivities if they get hungry.

To organize the meal, talk to the chefs of the family. You may want to create a potluck event where everybody brings something, prepare everything at home with the help of the family, or have the ceremony catered.

On the next page is a menu with suggested ideas for delicious dishes that your guests may love.

Naming Ceremony Brunch

Molded Corn Sticks

Leah's Rice and Pecan Salad

Little Hands Mixed Salad

New Orleans Creole Chicken

West African Jollof Rice

Holiday Sweet-Potato Fries

Rice with Raisins

Fresh Fruit Mango Sorbet

Oatmeal-Raisin-and-Cranberry Bars

Tropical Sorrel Punch

Let Creativity Reign!

Whether you're naming an infant, a teenager, or an adult, you want the occasion to be special. This is truly a great family celebration. Give yourself time to consider different ways that you can infuse the event with your family's love as you also make an interesting, dynamic activity for everyone. Here are some ideas:

Celebrating Your Name

Invite your child to create an empowering birthday ritual. Each year, she can research her name to discover new meanings. She can read African history books to learn about others who have carried her name. What about visiting art galleries that feature art from the part of the world where her name originates? After conducting research, the child can make an art project that illustrates this year's naming lesson. Ideas include:

- Writing and performing a short play with siblings or friends, the child enacts a story about the meaning of his or her name.
- Write poems illustrating the great qualities inherent in those carrying the name.
- Write a story about a character with the child's name who goes from one grade to the next, with the child.
- Write a song that celebrates your name.

Craft: Make Name Banners

Focus on your name and celebrate it with a banner or flag.

What You Need:

- Squares of colored felt
- Stencil
- Pencil
- Scissors
- Glue
- Sticks
- Stapler
- Glitter (optional)

Getting Started:

1. Using the stencil, trace letters of your name or that of the person being named on a piece of felt.
2. Carefully cut out the traced letters.

A name banner is a useful craft to make, in that it reminds the child to value the name she or he has been given.

3. Position the cutout letters on a square of felt in another color.

4. Glue the letters to the felt. Allow to dry, about 20 to 30 minutes.

5. Take another piece of plain felt to use as a backing. Put the glued felt over the backing felt and place a stick in between.

6. Staple along both sides of the stick, securing it to the felt.

Craft: Make a Name Quilt

Making a quilt can be a great long-term creative project. Make one bearing your name or that of a new family member.

What You Need:
- Fabric squares
- Cotton batting
- Stencil
- Pencil
- Needle and thread
- Sewing machine (optional)
- Quilt pattern book (optional)

Getting Started:
1. Using your stencil, cut out letters that spell the name along with its meaning. You may want to cut out other words that represent the love you have for the person being named too.

2. Design your own pattern for your quilt, such as simple boxes sewn together or a more detailed pattern.

3. Begin by sewing the pieces together by hand.

4. Once you have the top of the quilt sewn together, decide where you will place the letters and words, and sew them on top of the quilt top, making an interesting shape.

5. Sew pieces together for the back of the quilt, and put more words on the back if you like.

6. Place cotton batting between the front and back of the quilt and sew the two together along the outer edges, turning the selvage inside to make smooth seams.

7. If you have a sewing machine, you can use it to enclose the batting and then sew patterns across the quilt to capture the stuffing. If you have not made a quilt before, use a pattern.

Craft: Personalize Thank-you Cards

When you want to say thank you, do it with a personal touch, using cards with your indentification on them.

What You Need:
- Square or rectangular pieces of card stock—flat or folded (available at an arts-and-crafts store)
- Colorful markers
- Matching envelopes

Getting Started:
1. Use markers to write the name in creative ways on the outside of your card stock.

2. You can write *Thank You* beneath the name or save it for the inside.

3. If the card folds, you can write *Thank You* in the middle, leaving space for the family to inscribe a personal message.

Craft: Personalize a Cake

If you're a good baker, by all means make a cake to celebrate the naming. Whether you make it from scratch or buy a delicious cake from a local baker, be sure to inscribe it with the new name. If you do it at home, the whole family can join in the fun.

What You Need:
- A fully baked and cooled cake
- Frosting
- Colored cake paint

Getting Started:
1. Ice your cake with the base color and let it sit for about 20 minutes.

2. Squeeze your colored cake paint onto the cake spelling the name of the celebrant.

3. You can add hearts or other symbols of love and prosperity to finish the decoration around the name.

Most important for a naming ceremony is to make concerted efforts to acknowledge the power of the name and its relationship to the one bearing it. Rejoice in the child bearing this great name and welcome this great being into a life of happiness.

Welcome your loved one to the world with a personalized cake. This one, designed by baker Charmaine Jones, features edible conch shells and African symbols.

chapter four

family reunions

Nurturing Generational Ties

From the sign welcoming the family members to a photomontage of those past and present, take the time to make your reunion special.

J OHN AND I WENT TO HISTORIC CAMP ATWATER IN NORTH BROOKFIELD, Massachusetts, a couple of years ago to talk to the campers about the special events that they love to attend with their families. At the top of most of the young campers' lists was their family reunion. It sounded like these people, who represented neighborhoods all over the country, loved getting together with their families, catching up with their cousins, and just having a great time. One teenage girl was born in Zimbabwe and now lives in the United States. When her family gets together, they come from all over the world. A ten-year-old boy spoke of his reunion and how he has the chance to arm wrestle with the other boys his age, swim, and just hang out all day long.

The pursuit of fun drove all of these children's interests. Having a great time with family made it all the more special, because it happens more and more rarely. So, how can you have fun with your family and make it count? Included in this chapter are all sorts of ideas for families to work together in advance to iron out all the details of the reunion, and things you can do at the reunion to make it the best fun of all.

Why It's Important

We already know that children love to see one another. Indeed a family reunion represents the one time that some families get to be together—usually in warm weather—to share their love. As with each of the other activities in *Coming Together*, the family reunion is an event set aside by the choice of the family to honor its members. Even when various members are busy living their lives, managing their jobs, soccer practices, births, and deaths, the family reunion can and does serve as an anchor for so many. It represents a reserved space in time when everyone chooses to recognize their love for one another and strengthen that bond together. The planning of the reunion often gets folks to thinking about who the family is, how many limbs of the family tree exist. Out of that curiosity many wonderful discoveries have been made of cousins, aunts, uncles, and property that no one imagined existed.

Your Family Tree: Researching Your Family Lineage

Today there are many options for researching your family history. And yes, despite slavery and what it did to our families, many of us can still trace our histories pretty far back. What we often find is that we have a mixture of cultures that make up our families, including people of African descent from all over the United States, many different groups of Native Americans, West Indians, Africans, and Europeans. It will take some effort to find out about all of your links. Here are some of the things you can do:

- Look up your family names and history on the Web and surf for genealogy

Web sites that will help you with your research. One of the most comprehensive sites is www.ancestry.com. This site has useful information like links to sites where you can conduct searches of public records and software to help you create a family tree. Also, see www.cyndislist.com, which will direct you to many valuable sources of information.

- Write to the Library of Congress for information about your family. The library is located at 101 Independence Ave., SE, Washington, DC 20540. The Library of Congress is the second-largest library in the world, with more than 120 million items, including more than 18 million books, 12 million photographs, and 54 million manuscripts. You can search some of the library's archives online, but ultimately you may have to make a visit there to do specific, detailed research. For more information, visit the library's Web site at www.loc.gov or call 202-707-5000.

- Invite family members to contribute to a genealogy fund. The costs of research can add up. You can make the donation optional or structure it into your reunion dues, if you have them.

- Design a Web site that documents your family tree. Then your entire family can refer to it during the course of the year. You can ask family members to send you information they learn about family members that you can add to missing limbs on the family tree.

Planning Your Reunion

Because people often travel hundreds or thousands of miles for their reunions, many families are organizing events that span several days. Naturally, this means that there needs to be more planning to accommodate travelers. One family, the Arnolds, who have relatives from Atlanta, Los Angeles, and Chicago, have figured out a great solution. They hold their reunion every two years, alternating between the East and West coasts, with the applicable host committees having responsibilities to plan and execute the events. The committees make sure there's plenty to do over a four- or five-day period. Lots of kids come to the reunions, so they always find a special activity for them, such as visiting a theme park, as well as board games and sports activities.

For many families, the annual reunion is the one time a year—or however often they host one of these grand events—when loved ones gather together. Because so many of us move away from the city where we grew up, going to a family reunion often requires travel, a long drive with family in tow or a flight to reach the destination. That means that all of the various family members need to know details about the reunion far enough in advance to properly plan.

Still, for most of the people who come, the family reunion is one great day or an extended weekend at best. For a few it means a lot of work in advance. Indeed, the preparation for a successful family reunion can begin months, even years, before the actual event.

Someone must keep track of the roster of names and addresses in order to invite folks to come. The location has to be confirmed, especially if the reunion is being held in a public park or other facility that needs a special permit. Menus need to be determined. Activities and supporting props for them defined. Accommodations must be arranged for out-of-town family members. Sometimes they can stay with other relatives. Depending upon how many people are coming and what the family accommodations are like, you may need to research

Some of the most precious moments during a family reunion occur when you're just being together. Learning from one another and sharing your love.

hotels. What's great is that most hotels allow you to negotiate special deals for large groups. Again this is a task for somebody to tackle early on. And so the list of responsibilities expands. Like every other event, a family reunion is a big production. You can be a part of coordinating the festivities from the start. And, even if you and your family are not able to work from the ground up, your presence at the reunion will do wonders for making it a great event.

Design a Village-Style Family Reunion

My mother's parents' families are from Calvert County, Maryland, a small county in the southern part of the state about forty-five miles from Washington, D.C. More than thirty years ago, the families decided to host family reunion celebrations where everyone would come together as one. The Freelands (my grandfather's family), the Sewells (my grandmother's people), and the Rays and Morsells (cousins) agreed on a date and started preparing menus. One cousin found a nice park and reserved a plot for picnicking and playing. Somebody else was assigned to reach out to family members who were living in the "city" (Baltimore) and other parts of the country, to invite them. And it's been going strong every since.

What's more, several cousins decided they wanted to learn more about the individual families and how they were blood connected. My cousin Tawana Fisher's inspiration turned into more than twenty years of research in the National Archives, the Library of Congress, and other national registries. During lunch hours at her job in D.C. and on weekends, she put together much of the puzzle of our family history. As a result, at each reunion she has brought more information and clues about who the Calvert County families really are.

You can do the same things that these families have done. If you have a small family and you want to create a livelier event, expand your circle. In older communities, neighbors become almost like family when multiple generations live side by side. When you do your research, you may be surprised to find that some of your neighbors actually are your relatives now—by blood or by marriage.

Panamanian Style

Some folks have expanded their definition of family to include those who may not be related by blood or marriage, but who have other ties, such as culture and homeland. In 1984, several members of the family who had immigrated from Panama some years earlier met to talk about how they could spend more quality time together. They had moved to the United States from their homeland, and as much as they enjoyed their new life, they missed the close ties of family members. Out of their discussion came a small gathering. Being together was so great that they decided to do it again. Nearly two decades later, their gathering has mushroomed into a huge event that welcomes the original families as well as all families of Panamanian descent living in the United States.

The National Panamanian Friendship Reunion has become a fun and empowering event for the more than 2,700 people who attend each year. In addition to arts-and-crafts activities for the children, the reunion hosts workshops for teenagers and adults, and they bring in qualified speakers to share their knowledge with everyone. The range of activities is broad, including workshops on money management, applying for college, and health care. Best of all, the reunion requires a nominal registration fee, part of which goes to a scholarship fund for family members. For more information, check out the National Panamanian Friendship Reunion Web site www.panamanianreunion.org.

Getting together with family can be as simple as gathering at one home to spend time in each other's company. The Haitian families Mith and Ganthier, and others, cherish this time.

The Pinderhughes Gathering: A Special Event

Although John and Victoria Pinderhughes don't usually have family reunions, they did in the fall of 1998. Forty members of the Pinderhughes family showed up at their home in Sag Harbor for three full days of activities. In addition to their home, they rented five other houses on the island to accommodate their family. Everybody gathered for meals, which included group cooking and cleaning. The family spent three fun-filled days playing softball and tennis, swimming, fishing, kayaking, playing cards, and going on nature walks. John explains: "We spent a lot of time just getting reacquainted with each other and being delighted that our children bonded so quickly." What's more, the adults participated in an African ritual of calling on the spirits. They stood in a circle and called the names of deceased family members whose spirits they wanted to remember and revere.

You can do the same. Make plans when you are inspired to bring family together. Pay attention to all the details so that you can make the event the best possible. Think of special activities that will bring your family members closer together, that will create beautiful memories for everyone. A single event can have long-lasting meaning for every member of your family. Maybe next year another limb of your family tree will be inspired to host another event.

Family Reunion Fun: Games

Chances are you know some of your cousins, while others you will meet for the first time at your reunion. When you meet new people, it takes a minute to get comfortable with them, doesn't it? Since you know this already, why not come up with some cool activities that will make it easier for you to break the ice? Consider these ideas:

- **The Name Game:** A classic camp game. Have everyone sit in a circle. One person starts by saying his name. The next person says the first person's name plus his own name. The next person has three names to say, and so on, all the way around. This is a fun game where the list gets as long as the number of people in the circle. If a person forgets a name, he has to go to the end of the circle and get another try, which means he will have to remember more names.

- **Hot Peas and Butter:** This game is a classic. The more players you have, the better. Hot peas and butter is a form of hide-and-seek, except that in this game you need an object to hide, such as a family baseball or miniature photo album. Players hide their eyes while a designated person hides the object. No peeking! After the object has been safely hidden, the person yells, "Hot peas and butter!" All the players now are on a hunt to go recover the object. If players gets close to the object, the person who hid it can let them know by telling them they're "Hot." If they're not close he or she says, "Cold." If the players get too far away or close to the object, the player who hid it can say "Warmer" or "Colder." The first person to find the object gets to hide it next. At the end of the game, if you use an object that is important to the family, you can all sit around and share stories about its meaning. If it's a small photo album, you can add photos from this year's event to it.

- **Steal the Bacon:** This game can be played with any number of people, but is best played with teams of equal size. Find an object to be used as the

Family photos are a must at reunions.

Above: The Calvert County families reunion in the mid 1970s, featuring my family.

Opposite: John's 1998 grand event for the Pinderhughes clan.

bacon, such as a stick, rolled-up newspaper, or a relay baton. Have the teams line up facing each other, with a wide space between them. Each team member gets a number that matches an opposing player on the other team. Now, the bacon is placed in the middle of both teams, and the scorekeeper yells out a number and/or numbers. The players of each team assigned to those numbers will run out to grab the bacon. The first player to snatch up the bacon and bring it back to the team without being tagged by the opposing team wins a point! You can decide on how many points it takes to win the game.

Don't forget about the younger children. Check in on them periodically to make sure they're having fun too. When it makes sense you can invite them to participate in games with the adults and older kids. Here are some fun outdoor games that are great for older and younger kids to do together:

- Human Wheelbarrow: This is a race that requires two partners to make each team. The smaller partner (younger brother or sister or cousin) places his or her hands on the ground, while the taller partner holds onto the smaller one's feet. Together, the pairs of teams race each other to the finish line.

- Tug-of-War: Okay, for this game to be fair, you have to divide up so that there's a balance of strength between two teams. Older and younger kids have to mix. You may want to divide up by different family names or in other creative ways. Using a long rope, the game is made more challenging by standing over a puddle of water or some other crevice that will make it obvious when there is a winner and a loser. Pull to your heart's content.

- Family Charades: Everybody can play this game, from grandparents to young children. Make the focus of this game acting out illustrations of different family members whose personalities are relatively easy to recognize. You can have lots of fun as you also learn about the different members of your extended family. You can also illustrate simple stories of your family's history.

- Pictionary: You can create your version of this popular game by coming up with ideas to illustrate through drawing that document features of your family's heritage. What a great way to get to know each other and remind one another of what makes your family unique!

Teen Time: Host a Face-Painting Clinic

Creative teens can have a blast taking care of younger kids with this activity. You do need to organize yourself in advance. Shop for water-based paint that is safe for use on the skin. You can find all kinds of paint and brushes that will work at your local arts-and-crafts store. When you set up your workstation, make sure you have enough water and paper cups to clean your brushes each time you use them.

Think in advance of small-scale designs that children will like. You can practice on white paper to perfect your skill at drawing them. Then when you're working on the little ones the project will be a breeze. Favorites include flowers, stars, peace signs, and ladybugs.

Children love creative activities, especially face painting. Teenagers can lead a clinic that they invite all the young children to attend.

Form a Storytelling Circle

Now, you know that your Uncle Ted loves to tell stories. So does your Grandma Myrtle. Not to mention your younger brother Sam. Swapping family tales is fun, especially when you can tell brief stories that some folks call "tales out of school," those moments that are funny but that some would like to forget.

During the reunion, get together with family members and sit around in a circle. This makes it easy for everybody to see and hear one another. Go from one person to the next sharing memories of youth or other family moments that will paint a picture about your family and bring lots of laughter too. You never know what you'll learn. It would be perfect for an adult family member—even a teen— to record the stories and put them together in a family story collection to be shared next year.

Host an Auction

You know all that old stuff your family has lying around the house? Well, consider bringing it to your family reunion for a special family auction. Lots of families do this these days. It's really simple.

1. Bring a range of items that you no longer want or need that could be of value to others—such as old books, family photos, mementos from trips, clothing.

2. Make sure you have a microphone. If anybody in the family has a karaoke machine, that would work perfectly.

3. Make auction paddles—you can use wooden sticks glued to stiff paper such as construction paper—with numbers on them for those who plan to bid on items. Young people can be in charge of making these before the event. One side can say the family name, the other side a number.

4. Have a cash box with ample change.

5. Assign someone who is entertaining and speaks clearly to be the auctioneer.

6. Have fun. Make sure that those who have offered items write down little stories about the things they have brought. In this way, the auctioneer gets to share great family history throughout the auction. For example, when he is introducing a pair of baby booties, he can explain that these belonged to the patriarch of the family. Everybody will love that!

7. Create a family reunion fund with a bank. The proceeds from the auction can be used to pay for the rentals and other costs of the reunion. They may also be used for a family scholarship fund, a pool of money that can support young people as they head off to pursue higher education.

Showcase Family Heritage

For years the family of Lou Scott Brown, a friend of John's, has gathered at Brown's house on Sunday afternoons following church. Occasionally, they get together in larger numbers for a reunion. In the summer of 2000, about 200 family members converged at a park near Lou's Maryland home, where there was plenty of room for everybody to have a great time.

Father time with children is essential to their development and happiness. During your reunion, make sure that the dads get time alone with their little ones.

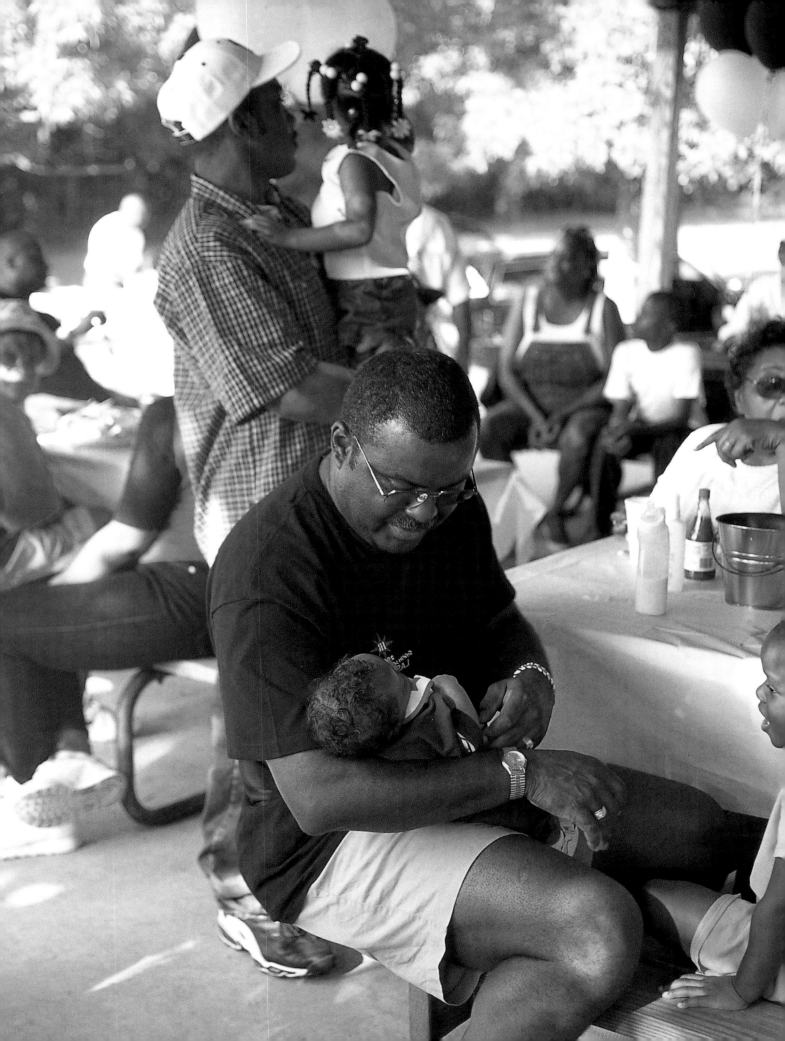

of room for everybody to have a great time.

Because the family has so much history, they decided to bring along elements to remind old and young of who belongs to the family. Lou and her daughter, Laureen Offer, worked with a small team of family members to organize the logistics for the event. Before this reunion, they made up poster boards with collages of family images creating a gallery for everyone to view. Everybody was really excited to visit the gallery that they had set up under a tent in the park.

You can easily do this for your family, and it's a great project for young people to champion. Call your various family members and ask them to send photos that show everyone from their home in different stages of their lives. Be sure to ask for photos of the eldest members of your family, especially if anyone has pictures of them when they were young. Ask for the names and years of the photos to be written on the back. When you receive the photos, you can record the information in a ledger and then affix them in creative ways to poster board or oak tag. You can also create a written document that serves as a guide through the photo gallery. Each year as new pictures are taken at the reunions, you can add to your living visual document of the family.

In addition to the photos in your gallery, you can include historic family memorabilia. At Bebe Granger's family reunion, relatives have showcased all sorts of treasures, from framed manumission papers to vintage family diplomas. Other families have show-and-tell with birth certificates, diaries of relatives long passed (encased in a clear box and opened to a great page for reading), arts-and-crafts projects that little ones have made, and so on.

If there's an indoor area that's part of your reunion, you may want to include a video portion in your gallery. You can show video footage from the last family reunion. Perhaps someone in the family is good at editing film. Then you can include footage that you collect from many family members that you turn into a special video for next year.

Organize a Slumber Party

Many family reunions last three or more days. Because many people travel long distances with children, there's always a question of how adults and children can relax during the reunion. Why not give the teens some responsibility? They can organize a slumber party for the younger children, taking baby-sitting to a new level! Family members can pitch in to rent a suite for the night for all the young people. You can buy foodstuffs at a local grocery store to save on expenses. Make sure you have lots of fun games to occupy each age group.

Because months or even a whole year may have passed since the children have seen one another—and some kids may be new to the group—start out with some introductory activities. The group can play guessing games as they try to remember interesting facts about their cousins from the previous year.

It may work well to divide the children up into age groups or gender groups, depending upon how they get along. One family organized the girls ages seven to thirteen and planned a dress-up party. A few weeks ahead of the reunion, all of the young girls were contacted and invited to bring their favorite outfits so that they could participate in a family-reunion fashion show. When they all arrived, the girls were giddy with excitement about the upcoming activities. While their parents were enjoying the banquet, they were in the hotel suite trying on clothes and planning how they were going to walk their "runway." The next day, the girls staged a fashion show complete with music courtesy of the teenager assigned to play CDs. Everybody had a great time. Because two of the teens decided to videotape the event, they have it in their records.

Don't forget the boys during slumber party time. Their ages will dictate what they want to do the most, but often it has to do with cars, trucks, and building. More and more, computer games figure in as well. For young boys, why not design a contest with their favorite toys. You can clear away space to make a racetrack where the boys bring their favorite cars and race them for a prize. Be sure to create categories for the children with hand-powered cars as well as remote-control versions. For computer-game buffs, plan ahead and ask parents and children to bring several laptops that can be set up as computer stations. Plan competitions with the same games that the boys can play simultaneously, again with fun prizes as incentives.

These ideas may work for your family, or you may have others. What's important at a slumber party is that everybody feels included, that you have a bounty of activities and snacks to keep children occupied, and that you have ample supervision. Or you can gather them all at a family member's home—the one with the most space—and just make all the food there.

Stage a Talent Show

Author Sobonfu Somé talks about the importance of community in nurturing the gifts of its members. In her book *The Spirit of Intimacy* she talks about the role of the community in welcoming the bounty of talents that each member has to offer. Only when people feel that their contributions are appreciated do they feel inspired to offer them.

This is why it's so great when family members are gathered to let loved ones showcase their talents. Young and old can get into the spirit of the event. In advance, the coordinator of the reunion can contact families letting them know the details—time limits for talent presentation, content parameters and rehearsal schedule. At the Cunningham Family Reunion in Delaware each year, the talent show is the most popular feature of the Saturday night family banquet. The show takes place during a break in the meal when everybody can pay close attention. Every participant gets a thank-you gift and one gets a grand prize. The event is great fun—and it serves the important role of sharing love.

Serve a Family Reunion Feast

At every great family reunion you can smell the scent of food wafting in the air, because people started working on the meal well before the big day. You may have helped your family to prepare special items, or you may choose to help out once you arrive. There are several ways young people can help with the meal:

- Help Grandma shuck corn before it goes in the huge pot of boiling water.
- Get a lesson on grilling from Uncle Lester.
- Help set up the buffet table with flatware, napkins, cups, and condiments.

Plan a Surprise Activity
Tracie Howard's family always plans a surprise for the last night of their reunion, which ends with a formal dinner dance. At their most recent reunion, Howard explained, "The family ended their festivities by offering every person a souvenir reunion mug. The host committee had had the mugs specially designed—each with a different family member's name on it. Each family member randomly picked a mug and then announced whose name was on it. Whoever was on that mug was to be the person's 'special cousin.'" Over the course of the year, the two were to be in contact—on birthdays, other holidays, or just to catch up. In this way, cousins who don't normally talk to each other have a chance to get close.

A Family Reunion Feast

Black-Skillet Corn Bread

Little Hands Mixed Salad

Your Grandma's Potato Salad

Aunt Betty's Maryland Fried Chicken

Charlie P's Fried Fish

Big Ma's Barbecued Salmon

Fresh Sweet Corn on the Cob

Sweet-Potato–Stuffed Apples

Celebration Spinach

Assorted Cold-Cut Sandwiches

Aunt M's Peach Cobbler

Ice Cream

Iced Tea Punch

Let Creativity Reign!

As you prepare for your family reunion, let your creative juices flow. Below are ideas culled from many families across the country that you may want to borrow.

Craft: Make Family Flags

Be enterprising. Imagine how much fun it can be to arrive at your family reunion with flags that salute the different families that have come together. In advance of the reunion, get together with your brothers and sisters and maybe some of your cousins. You can design a large family flag and smaller ones that each of you can carry as you arrive at the reunion.

What You Need

- Large squares of felt in the colors of your choice
- Wooden sticks (found in art-supply stores)
- Fabric glue
- Scissors
- Stapler
- Stencil for letters
- Pencil

Getting Started

1. Choose two pieces of felt, lay them flat, and cut across to make a triangle. This will be the background of your flag.
2. Choose another piece of felt in a different color for your letters. You may want to use more than one color for letters—a great idea.
3. Using the stencil, trace letters onto the felt with your pencil. Cut out the letters.
4. Use your fabric glue to attach your letters to your flag, spelling out your family name. Let dry before going to the next step—about 20 minutes.
5. Attach both pieces of your flag on both sides of the stick. Use the stapler to staple the felt on each side of the stick to hold it in place.
6. Now you have your own personal family flag.

Craft: Design Family Reunion T-Shirts

One of the most popular features of a family reunion is the T-shirt that links everyone together. Usually somebody is in charge of this project, which includes selecting the actual T-shirt, deciding on what it's going to say, picking a place that can reproduce it, and making enough for everyone who plans to attend. This is a great project for teens. Ask your parents if they will work with you to head up that team. With their guidance, you can come up with an interesting logo—a design that reflects your family's personality. Use the Yellow Pages to find a local printer who knows how to print on T-shirts and may even be a great source for purchasing T-shirts in bulk. Ask your parents to finance your venture. You will have to pay in advance for the T-shirts and printing, which you can later sell at a small profit at the reunion. Work with your parents to determine the retail price (what you will charge) and also your marketing strategy (how you will get the word out to others that you will have family reunion T-shirts for sale). Be sure to pay your parents back in full for their investment. (This way they'll be happy to finance your next venture.) Contribute 10 percent of your profits to the Family Reunion Fund for next year.

Getting Started

1. Find out how many people will attend your reunion and how many T-shirts are needed in different sizes for men, women, and children. Select a maximum number of five shirt sizes to order: XL, L, M, S, and a children's M.
2. You may want to choose a 100-percent cotton T-shirt, because 100-percent cotton wears better than cotton blends.
3. Work with the printer to come up with a design that will be exciting and fresh.
4. Decide exactly what the shirt will say. Make sure that you spell every

word correctly. Double-check with a dictionary and your parents to be sure.

5. Reserve a freestanding banquet table or a picnic table for sales. Bring a tablecloth to cover the table. This will keep the shirts clean.

6. Place your table at the entrance to your reunion so that everyone will see them as they walk in.

7. Make sure you have a cash box with enough change to make transactions easy.

8. Assign one teen to talk to customers while someone else handles actual sales.

Get Your Reunion on Film

Wouldn't it be great to record everything that happens at your family reunion this year? Ask your parents to teach you how to use the family video camera so that you can record the going-ons. (You can also hand out disposable cameras—as some people do at weddings—and let guests take photos.) Practice making videos at home so that you learn how to handle the camera and keep it still. Learn how to attach your camera to a tripod for longer interviews. This makes it possible for you to set your camera down on a table or other surface, so that you don't have to hold it. It also keeps your camera completely still. Here are a few pointers on how to document the whole event and get your family members to share their stories:

What You Need

- A handheld video camera (that you borrow from your parents)
- Several 60- or 90-minute videotapes
- Extra batteries
- A tripod (optional for longer interviews)

Getting Started

1. When you arrive at your family reunion, look around to see the whole landscape. Is there a family banner hanging? Are there different areas where activities are going on?

2. Start filming by documenting where you are. Take a close-up picture of the family banner and then span out to show the grounds for the reunion. Move slowly from left to right taking in the whole scene.

3. If your camera also records sound, you can narrate as you go along. Say your name and the date and where you are exactly. Describe what you are seeing as you take in the scenery. As you notice people, say who they are and what their relationship is to you.

4. Pause in your filming by using the PAUSE button. Whenever you want to stop and look, pause rather than stopping the camera. This will make your film easier to look at later.

5. Pay attention to what's happening. Is there an area where people are grilling food? Setting up picnic tables? Playing ball and other games? Sitting around and talking? Fanning themselves in the heat? Look and see what's interesting to you.

6. Notice who's at the reunion. You will probably see several groups of people: the older folks—grandparents, aunts and uncles; your parents' and your cousins' parents; teenagers, children.

7. After you have taken in the whole scene, decide where to go first. You may want to invite one of your cousins or a brother or sister to work with you. You can start out by filming the scene from a distance. Then go in closer and interview people briefly.

8. Your assistant can be the interviewer, asking people to state their names, their ages, and a short story about the family.

9. When you get to the older people, give yourself more time. They like to tell stories that often last a little longer. As they are talking, zoom in and out. Notice what's interesting about their environment and about them. If your grandmother is shucking corn while talking, zoom in on her

hands and that activity as she speaks. In this way, your film will be more dynamic.

10. Be sure to capture any games that your family plays—relay races, volley-ball, baseball, and family trivia games.

11. Videotape the food before people start eating. Be sure to show the people who are preparing the food. You can ask them what the menu is and how they prepared certain dishes that look great.

12. If other people start taking pictures with cameras, you can videotape the group shots as they are happening. Stand back a little, so you can get the photographers in your shot. Remember to move around. Videotape captures movement and sound!

13. When you get home, ask your parents to help you edit and copy your film. If you have the software, you may be able to add a title that says it's your family reunion and music.

14. Here's a chance for another enterprise. Find a wholesaler who will sell you videotapes and make copies for you. Then figure out a price that covers your expenses plus a small profit and offer the videotape to your loved ones so that everybody can remember your great celebration.

For more information on documenting a special event, see "Document Your Events," page 118.

Craft: Make a Memory Book

A great way to capture special bonds made during the family reunion is to invite people to write down their thoughts and affix photos later that document your event. Make this memory book to store those messages.

What You Need
- Colored construction paper
- Glue
- Hole puncher
- Notebook or ring binder
- Brown paper or cloth for cover
- Pencil
- Silver or gold pens (for notes and signatures)

Getting Started

1. Separate the colored construction paper by color. Take 2 pieces of paper that are the same color. Lay them on a piece of heavy cardboard and cut out a shape; making it just big enough to go around a photo. You can cut out circles, ovals, squares, rectangles, and other shapes.

2. Now glue the 2 sheets together, being careful to leave an edge on the side or top near your cutout to slide the photos in.

3. While these sheets are drying, take the brown paper and crumple it up. Then lay the paper out.

4. Place the ring binder or notebook on the crumpled paper. Trace around the notebook, leaving about 3 inches to fold over and glue.

5. Cut out the cover and glue into the notebook.

6. Take a sheet of unused construction paper and place over the pasted-down edges inside your notebook. Glue this paper down so that it all looks neat.

7. Collect your framing sheets of construction paper and punch holes in the correct edge. Place them in your notebook.

8. Cut out letters for the front of what has now become your memory book.

9. Take pictures of family at your reunion. Have family members write in the memory book. Use the special silver and gold pens for this. Later you can add the photos of each member of your family

The reason that families gather for reunions is to rekindle their bonds. Even so, many people have said that they have great fun at the event but don't always follow up later. Why not have the teens travel around the reunion site with guest books? They can invite every person present to write down name, address, phone number, birthday, and e-mail address, if they have one. Perhaps one of the industrious teens can create a family Web site that loved ones can visit for news and updates about what's happening, such as births, birthdays, promotions, moves, and more. You can keep your family close all year long just by thinking ahead and being creative. Conclusion: keep in touch.

family celebration recipes

ONE OF THE GREATEST JOYS OF GATHERING FOR SPECIAL FAMILY EVENTS IS EATING TOGETHER. AND BOY, DO WE KNOW how to make some delicious feasts! During the holidays, folks are famous for bringing out family specialties, like Grandma T's famous casserole and Uncle Freddie's barbecued ribs. Aunt Audrey contributed her famous corn pudding, and Aunt Esther chopped up some mixed salad like nobody's business.

Recipes are like family heirlooms; they're precious. From one generation to the next, relatives hand them down so that we can all enjoy the love and care that have gone into developing them over the years.

Ask your loved ones to make their favorite family recipes for your next family celebration. Plan a holiday preparation party where you get together and swap recipes, all the while sharing more stories from your family's history. Be sure to write down each other's recipes in a special book that you can add to all year long. When you display your meal, make place cards that attribute the names of the recipes and how they came into the family. Then as you're eating, share memories of your loved ones with everyone present.

Here are some favorite recipes that we gathered from families across the country. All of these recipes are easy to prepare, which makes them perfect for family cooking. Little ones can join in even if they may just be able to help pull out pots and pans or stir. Most of the recipes are safe for children who are eight or nine years old when carefully supervised. The idea is for families to make the meal together. When that's your focus, everybody really can pitch in, and it will be great. *Bon appétit!*

Measurement Abbreviations

Measurements are often listed in an abbreviated manner in recipes. Below are the standard abbreviations that we have used. Make sure that you use measuring spoons and cups that are accurately marked. That way your recipes will be delicious.

teaspoon=tsp.
tablespoon=tbsp.
pound=lb.
ounce=oz.
quart=qt.

**Other useful measurements
and information:**
a pinch=less than $1/8$ teaspoon
3 tsp.=1 tbsp.
2 tbsp.=1 fluid oz.
4 tbsp.= $1/4$ cup
8 tbsp.= $1/2$ cup
1 cup=8 fluid oz.
2 cups=1 pint
2 pints=1 qt.
1 qt.=32 fluid oz.
4 qts.=1 gallon
1 stick butter=8 tbsp.

Rules for Young People in the Kitchen

You'll have more fun and stay safe if you always follow these rules:

- Always get the permission and help of an adult—before you start to cook.
- Always wash your hands before beginning.
- As you work, keep your hands dry.
- Take your time; when you rush, accidents happen.
- Read the recipe carefully before you start.
- Assemble all your ingredients, then begin.
- Be very careful in the kitchen.
- Clean up as you go.
- Place only cooking pots on the stove.
- Always turn off the flame as soon as the dish is done.
- Always use pot holders to move the pots.
- Do not allow the handles to hang over the edge of the stove.
- Hold all kitchen tools by the handle.
- When cutting, always place ingredients on a cutting board.
- Get an adult to help you use a knife.
- Make sure your knife is sharp.
- Slice through your ingredient; do not just press down.
- Always keep fingers out of the way.
- Always clean up when you are finished.

STARTERS AND APPETIZERS

Coconut Chips

Equipment:
Hammer
Vegetable peeler
Large cast-iron skillet
Spatula

Ingredients:
1 ripe coconut
Salt to taste

Directions:
- Crack the coconut and save the liquid for another purpose. Crack the halves into pieces. Peel the brown rind away from the white meat.
- Using a vegetable peeler, slice the white meat into thin strips.
- Heat the skillet over low flame. Add coconut and toast gently until fragrant and slightly browned.
- Sprinkle with a little salt and serve.

Serves: 8

Plantain Chips

Equipment:
Knife
Cutting board
Large glass bowl
Medium-size cast-iron skillet
Box grater
Paper towels

Ingredients:
4 half-ripe plantains
2 tsp. salt
Water
Vegetable oil

Directions:
- Slice the ends off the plantains. Slice the plantains lengthwise, cutting just through the skin. Peel the plantains, discarding the skin.
- Slice the plantains into thin slices using the slicing side of a box grater, if available, or cut into thin slices with a knife.
- Soak the slices in a bowl of water to which 1 tsp. of salt has been added for 15 to 30 minutes.
- Heat vegetable oil in a medium-size cast-iron skillet to a depth of about $1^{1}/_{2}$ inches.
- Drain the plantain slices and dry them on paper towels.
- Fry plantains in small batches until they are golden brown, about 3 to 6 minutes, depending on thickness.
- Drain on paper towels and sprinkle liberally with salt.

Serves: 4

Black·Skillet Cornbread

Equipment:
Large glass bowl
Large cast-iron black skillet
Cooking spoon

Ingredients:
3 cups yellow cornmeal
$^{2}/_{3}$ cup all-purpose flour
4 tsp. baking powder
1 tsp. salt
$1^{1}/_{2}$ tsp. sugar
$1^{2}/_{3}$ cups buttermilk
2 eggs, beaten
5 to 6 tbsp. butter, melted
Dash of vanilla extract

Directions:
- Preheat oven to 400°.
- Place the cornmeal, flour, baking powder, salt, and sugar in a large bowl and mix well.
- Add the buttermilk, eggs, melted butter, and vanilla. Mix well.
- Butter a large cast-iron skillet and pour the batter into it.
- Place in preheated oven.
- Bake 20 to 30 minutes, until golden brown and firm to the touch.
- Set aside to cool. Bang the skillet once on a hard surface to loosen the cornbread.
- Serve hot, cut into wedges.

Serves: 6

Molded Corn Sticks

Equipment:
Large mixing bowl
Fork
Cast-iron corn stick molds

Ingredients:
1 cup yellow cornmeal
$^{1}/_{2}$ cup buttermilk
$^{1}/_{2}$ cup all-purpose flour
1 tbsp. butter, melted
1 tsp. sugar
1 egg, beaten
1 tsp. salt
1 tsp. baking powder
1 tsp. vegetable oil

Directions:
- Preheat oven to 400°.
- In a large mixing bowl, mix together the cornmeal, buttermilk, flour, butter, sugar, egg, salt, and baking powder.
- Brush the cast-iron molds with vegetable oil.
- Pour the cornmeal mixture into each

mold, filling about halfway.
- Place the molds in preheated oven.
- Bake about 15 to 20 minutes, until golden brown.
- Bang the mold on a hard surface to dislodge the corn sticks.

Serves: 4 (about 16 corn sticks)

Black-eyed Pea Fritters (Akara)

Equipment:
Large glass bowl
Electric blender
Knife
Cutting board
Large heavy pot
Paper towels

Ingredients:
1$\frac{1}{4}$ cups dried black-eyed peas ($\frac{1}{2}$ pound)
$\frac{1}{4}$ cup chopped onion
$\frac{1}{4}$ cup finely chopped pared fresh ginger
$\frac{1}{2}$ cup water
$\frac{1}{4}$ tsp. ground cayenne pepper
1 tsp. salt
Vegetable oil for deep frying

Directions:
- Place the black-eyed peas in a large bowl and cover with water. Allow the peas to soak overnight.
- Rub the peas between your hands until all the skins have been rubbed off. Drain the peas and rinse several times.
- Place the peas in a blender and add the onion, ginger, water, cayenne pepper, and salt. Blend until thick and smooth.
- Heat the oil in a large deep heavy pot, to a depth of about 2 inches, until the oil is hot but not smoking.
- Scoop up a rounded tablespoon of the pea mixture and drop it into the hot oil. Fry 6 to 8 pieces at a time, about 5 minutes, until golden brown. Drain on paper towels.

Makes: 24 fritters

Grandma T's Fresh Fruit Cup

Equipment:
Small paring knife
Large mixing bowl
Long-handled wooden spoon
Fruit-section knife or grapefruit knife

Ingredients:
2 large grapefruit
3 large oranges
1 small pineapple
2 bananas
2 Granny Smith apples
1 lb. green seedless grapes
2 small jars cherries
3 cups orange juice

Directions:
- Cut the grapefruit and oranges in half and scoop out the sections. Cut the skin off the pineapple and cut the meat into pieces. Peel and slice the bananas. Peel and core the apples; cut the apples in half and cut each half into 8 slices; coarsely chop the slices. Cut the grapes in half. Cut the cherries in half.
- Place all the fruit in the mixing bowl and add the orange juice. Taste to make sure it is sweet enough. Add a little sugar, but only if necessary.

Serves: 8

SALADS

Leah's Rice and Pecan Salad

Equipment:
Small paring knife
Glass bowl

Ingredients:
3 cups leftover cooked rice
$\frac{1}{2}$ cup sliced scallions
$\frac{1}{2}$ cup chopped green bell pepper
$\frac{1}{2}$ cup chopped celery
3 tbsp. chopped parsley
1 cup pecans
2 tbsp. white wine vinegar
6 tbsp. olive oil
Salt to taste
Freshly ground pepper to taste

Directions:
Combine all ingredients in the glass bowl and season to taste.

Serves: 8

Avocado and Ginger Salad

Equipment:
Small paring knife
Cutting board
Medium glass bowl

Ingredients:
1 large ripe avocado
$\frac{1}{2}$ large lemon
$\frac{1}{2}$ tsp. ground ginger, or more to taste
$\frac{1}{2}$ tsp. salt
Sliced tomatoes
Sliced red onion

Directions:
- Cut the avocado in half and remove the seed. Pull the skin from the avocado.
- Cut the avocado into $\frac{1}{2}$-inch cubes and place them in the bowl.
- Squeeze the lemon over the avocado and sprinkle with the ginger and salt. Toss gently and cover. Set aside to marinate for 15 to 20 minutes.
- Garnish with sliced tomatoes and red onion.
- Serve immediately.

Serves: 4

Old-fashioned Apple Chicken Salad

Equipment:
Small paring knife
Medium saucepan with top
Large mixing bowl
Long-handled wooden spoon

Ingredients:
2 chicken breasts
1 Granny Smith apple
1 lemon
1 cup chopped celery
$3/4$ cup red seedless grapes, halved
$1/2$ cup coarsely chopped pecans
1 tsp. salt
$1/2$ tsp. freshly ground pepper
$1 1/2$ cups mayonnaise

Directions:
- Place the chicken breasts in the saucepan and add about an inch of water. Cover and bring to a boil. Reduce the flame to low and poach 15 minutes, or until just done. Drain the chicken and allow it to cool. When cool, remove skin and fat and discard. Cut the chicken into $1/2$-inch cubes. Set aside.
- Peel and core the apples. Cut into thick slices and then coarsely chop. As you cut up the apples, add to the mixing bowl. Squeeze lemon juice over the apples and turn to coat.
- When all the apples have been coarsely chopped, add the celery, grape halves, nuts, salt, pepper, and mayonnaise. Mix well.

Serves: 4 to 6

Black-eyed Pea and Rice Salad

Equipment:
Large glass bowl
Cooking spoon
Knife
Cutting board

Ingredients:
$1 1/2$ cups leftover cooked rice
16-oz. can black-eyed peas, drained and rinsed
3 large scallions, sliced
1 tbsp. chopped flat-leaf parsley
2 cloves garlic, minced
$1/2$ cup chopped red or green bell pepper
2 tsp. red wine vinegar

2 tbsp. olive oil
$1/2$ tsp. thyme leaves
$1/2$ tsp. salt
$1/2$ tsp. freshly ground black pepper

Directions:
- Let the rice come to room temperature. Fold into a large bowl, separating the rice grains with a fork.
- Add the black-eyed peas, scallions, parsley, garlic, bell pepper, red wine vinegar, olive oil, thyme leaves, salt, and pepper.
- Toss to mix well. Leave the salad to rest before serving to allow the flavors to meld.
- Toss again just before serving. Serve at room temperature or slightly chilled.

Serves: 4

Note: You can also make this salad without the rice and using more of the other ingredients.

Little Hands Mixed Salad

Equipment:
Small paring knife
Salad spinner
Large salad bowl

Ingredients:
1 head iceberg lettuce
1 head red-leaf lettuce
2 large cucumbers
5 ripe tomatoes
2 medium red onions
10 large radishes

Directions:
- Cut the lettuce in half and cut away the hard inner core. Tear the lettuce into pieces. Wash and spin dry. Put the lettuce in the salad bowl.
- Peel and slice the cucumbers. Core the tomatoes and cut into wedges. Thinly slice the onion. Thinly slice the radishes. Add to the lettuce. Toss to mix.
- Pour dressing (see below) over and toss.

Dressing:
$1/2$ cup olive oil
4 tbsp. balsamic vinegar
3 cloves garlic, finely chopped
2 tsp. Dijon mustard
1 tsp. anchovy paste
1 tsp. salt
$1/2$ tsp. freshly ground pepper
$1/2$ tsp. sugar

Directions:
Whisk together oil and vinegar; add all other ingredients, combining thoroughly.

Serves: 10 to 12

MAIN DISHES

New Orleans Creole Chicken

Equipment:
Large, deep casserole
Knife
Cutting board
Long-handled cooking fork

Ingredients:
4-lb. chicken, cut into 12 pieces
1 tsp. salt
$1/2$ tsp. freshly ground black pepper
$1/4$ cup vegetable oil
1 cup chopped onion
1 cup chopped green bell pepper
2 cups crushed tomatoes
2 cups water
2 cloves garlic, chopped
2 sprigs fresh thyme
$1/4$ tsp. cayenne pepper
12 whole okra
1 pound shrimp, shelled
1 tbsp. chopped parsley

Directions:
- Season the chicken all over with the salt and pepper.
- Heat the oil in the large casserole and add the chicken. Sauté the chicken, turning several times until it turns golden

104

Appetizers are essential for gatherings. Think about what serving dishes you will use and where you will place them. Make sure they are ready before your guests arrive. That way, even if you are still preparing the rest of your meal, guests have something yummy to eat.

Gettting children to eat salad can be tough, but when they help make it everything changes. Schedule a salad-making event with your children. Everybody washes hands together. Each one has an assignment: older children chop, younger ones wash and shred; everybody's contribution makes one great salad.

brown, about 15 minutes. Remove and set aside.

- Add the onions to the pot and sauté briefly. Add the green pepper and sauté 5 minutes. Add the tomatoes, water, garlic, thyme, cayenne, and another tsp. of salt.
- Simmer the sauce for 5 minutes; then return the chicken to the pot. Lower heat, cover, and cook 20 minutes.
- Add the okra and cook, uncovered, 10 minutes. Add the shrimp and cook until the shrimp turn pink, about 5 minutes. Add parsley. Serve with hot, cooked rice.

Serves: 6

West African Groundnut Stew

Equipment:
Knife
Cutting board
Paper towels
Small glass bowl
Large heavy casserole
Long-handled cooking fork

Ingredients:
4 to 6 lb. chicken, cut into 12 pieces
1 tsp. salt
1 tbsp. ground ginger
$1/2$ cup peanut or vegetable oil
1 cup chopped onion
28-oz. can tomato puree
2 tbsp. tomato paste
$1/4$ cup ground dried shrimp (see Note)
1 tsp. chopped garlic
1 tsp. minced peeled fresh ginger
$1/2$ tsp. red pepper flakes
$1/2$ tsp. freshly ground black pepper
6 cups boiling water
1 cup smooth peanut butter
1 cup cold water
12 fresh okra
6 hard-boiled eggs, shelled

Directions:
- Wash the chicken and remove excess fat. Pat dry with paper towels.
- Mix the salt and ground ginger in a

small bowl, then rub the mixture over the chicken.

- Heat the oil in a large, heavy casserole over a medium flame until hot. Add the chicken pieces several at a time and cook, turning several times, until they are golden brown.
- When each piece is cooked, remove to a plate and set aside. Continue cooking until all the chicken pieces are done.
- Pour off all but $1/4$ cup of the remaining oil. Add the onion and sauté 5 minutes, stirring to dislodge the browned particles on the bottom of the pot.
- When the onions have turned translucent, add the tomato puree, tomato paste, ground shrimp, garlic, ginger, red pepper flakes, and freshly ground black pepper.
- Bring the pot to a boil; reduce the flame to low and simmer uncovered for 5 minutes.
- Stirring constantly, pour in the boiling water. Return the chicken to the pot along with any liquid that has accumulated. Turn the chicken until evenly covered with sauce.
- Simmer uncovered over low flame for 15 minutes.
- Meanwhile, mix the peanut butter with the cup of cold water, then add to the pot.
- Add the okra and continue cooking over low flame for 1 hour. If the pot boils too hard, place the lid on loosely.
- Cook until the chicken is very tender. Add the hard-boiled eggs and simmer another 5 minutes to warm them. Serve with hot, cooked rice.

Serves: 6

Note: Dried shrimp can be found in markets that carry Asian ingredients.

West African Jollof Rice

Equipment:
Kitchen knife
Cutting board
Paper towels
Wooden cooking spoon
Long-handled cooking fork
Large heavy pot or casserole

Ingredients:
3 lb. chicken, cut into 12 pieces
$1^1/2$ lb. lean boneless beef, cut into cubes
2 tsp. salt
Freshly ground pepper to taste
6 tbsp. vegetable oil, for frying
2 medium onions, chopped
1 medium green bell pepper, seeded and chopped
2 medium carrots, chopped
14 green beans, cut into 1-inch lengths
28-oz. can tomatoes, drained and chopped
$1/4$ cup tomato paste
4 cloves garlic, chopped
1 hot pepper, to taste, seeded and chopped
1 tsp. grated peeled fresh ginger
1 bay leaf
1 tsp. thyme
4 cups chicken stock, fresh or canned
2 cups uncooked rice

Directions:
- Rinse the chicken pieces, removing all the fat. Pat dry with paper towels. Rinse the beef and pat dry. Sprinkle the chicken and beef pieces with salt and pepper.
- In a large heavy casserole, heat 3 tbsp. of vegetable oil. When the oil is hot, add the chicken, skin side down. Brown the chicken on all sides, about 5 minutes per side. Remove the browned chicken to a plate. Add the beef and brown on all sides. Remove and set aside.
- Pour off all but 2 tbsp. of oil. Add the onion and green pepper. Cook 5 minutes, making sure to scrape all the browned particles from the bottom of the pot. Add the carrots and green

beans and cook 5 minutes more. Add the tomatoes, tomato paste, garlic, hot pepper, ginger, bay leaf, and thyme. Increase the heat to high and stir to mix well. Cook, stirring, 10 minutes, until the sauce thickens.

- Add the chicken stock and the beef. Reduce the flame and simmer, partially covered, 30 minutes. Add the chicken and adjust seasonings. Simmer 10 minutes over a low flame.
- Stir in the rice, cover and cook 20 to 30 minutes, until the rice has absorbed all the liquid and the chicken and beef are done.

Serves: 6 to 8

Special Soy Roast Chicken

Equipment:
Small mixing bowl
Small paring knife
Box grater
Roasting rack
Roasting pan

Ingredients:
3- to 4-lb. chicken
1 lemon
$1/3$ cup soy sauce
$1/4$ cup olive oil
1 tbsp. sesame oil
1 tbsp. sherry
3 cloves garlic, finely chopped
1 tsp. salt
1 tsp. grated peeled fresh ginger
2 tsp. Chinese five-spice powder

Directions:
- Wash the chicken inside and out with cold water. Squeeze the lemon juice all over the chicken inside and out. Rinse the chicken again and pat dry with paper towels.
- Mix together the soy sauce, olive oil, sesame oil, sherry, garlic, salt, ginger, and 5-spice powder.
- Rub the chicken inside and out with the marinade. Push some of the marinade

under the skin. Place the chicken in a large plastic bag along with the marinade. Marinate 2 to 24 hours.
- Preheat the oven to 450°.
- Place the chicken on the roasting rack in the roasting pan and place in the oven. Roast 15 minutes, then reduce the heat to 350° and continue to roast 45–60 minutes, basting frequently. When the juices run clear, the chicken is done. Remove from oven and allow to rest for 20 minutes before carving.

Serves: 4 to 6

Charlie P's Fried Fish

Equipment:
Paper towels
Brown paper bag
Large glass bowl
Baking pan
Spatula
Fork
Large cast-iron skillet

Ingredients:
4 whole fish, heads removed, or large fillets, skin intact (catfish, croakers, porgies, or perch)
2 tsp. salt
$1 1/4$ cups all-pupose flour
2 tbsp. cold water
2 eggs, beaten
1 cup cornmeal
1 tsp. freshly ground black pepper
Vegetable oil, for frying

Directions:
- Rinse the fish under cold water. Pat dry with paper towels.
- Sprinkle a little salt over the fish, inside and out.
- Place 1 cup of flour in a paper bag and add the fish. Close the top of the bag and shake well until the fish is well coated.
- Add the cold water to the beaten eggs and mix well.
- Mix together the cornmeal, the $1/4$ cup of flour, 1 tsp. of salt, and the pepper. Place the mixture in a large shallow baking pan.

- Heat the vegetable oil in the cast-iron skillet. The oil will be hot enough when a small piece of bread browns in about 30 seconds.
- Dip the floured fish in the egg mixture and then in the cornmeal mixture, rolling it to cover completely.
- Fry the fish several pieces at a time, but do not overcrowd the skillet. Fry until the fish is golden brown, 4 to 5 minutes per side, depending on the size of the fish. Do not let the oil get too hot or the fish will burn. Drain the fish on paper towels.

Serves: 4

Baked Stuffed Fish Supreme

Equipment:
Paper towels
Large cast-iron skillet
Knife
Cutting board
Wooden cooking spoon
Large baking pan
Heavy-duty aluminum foil

Ingredients:
3- to 4-lb. whole fish (bluefish, red snapper, etc.), cleaned and split, backbone removed
Salt
Freshly ground pepper
8 tbsp. butter
1 small onion
$1/2$ small green bell pepper, seeded and chopped
1 rib celery, chopped
2 cloves garlic, chopped
$1/2$ lb. mushrooms, coarsely chopped
2 cups leftover cooked rice
1 medium onion, sliced
1 small green bell pepper, seeded and sliced
1 rib celery, sliced
1 large carrot, peeled and sliced
1 medium zucchini, sliced
1 tsp. thyme
1 cup fish stock

Aunt Betty's Maryland Fried Chicken

We love fried chicken! When it's made at home with loving care, it tastes oh-so-good. Teaching your children each step of the preparation will help them appreciate the delicious end result that much more. When frying, be sure to supervise children so they learn how to be careful at a hot stove.

Equipment:

Knife
Cutting board
Brown bag or large Ziploc bag
Long-handled cooking fork
Large cast-iron skillet

Ingredients:

1 frying chicken, cut into 8 pieces
2 cups all-purpose flour
2 tsp. paprika
2 tsp. Old Bay seasoning
2 tsp. salt
1 tsp. freshly ground black pepper
$1/2$ tsp. ground thyme
Vegetable oil for frying

Directions:

- Wash chicken and remove all excess fat.
- Place flour, paprika, Old Bay seasoning, salt, pepper, and thyme in a brown bag or large Ziploc bag. Shake to mix well.
- Add the chicken several pieces at a time and shake to coat with flour mixture. Set chicken pieces aside.
- Heat oil in a large cast-iron skillet to a depth of about $3/4$ inch. The oil will be hot enough when a small piece of bread browns in about 30 seconds.
- When the oil is hot, add the chicken several pieces at a time. Do not over-crowd the skillet. Cook about 20 minutes, turning several times until golden brown and cooked through.

Serves: 4

Directions:

- Preheat oven to 350°.
- Clean and wash the fish; pat dry. Sprinkle the fish inside and out with salt and pepper.
- Melt 2 tbsp. butter in a skillet. Add the chopped onion, green pepper, celery, and garlic. Sauté 5 minutes over a medium flame. Add the mushrooms and continue cooking about 5 minutes, until they begin to give up their liquid. Add the rice and remove from the stove. Mix well. Stuff the fish with the rice mixture.
- Grease the baking pan with a little butter. Place the fish in the baking pan. Scatter the sliced vegetables over and around the fish. Sprinkle with salt, pepper, and thyme.
- Cut the remaining butter into pats and place over the vegetables. Add the cup of fish stock. Cover with the aluminum foil.
- Place in preheated oven. Cook 30 to 40 minutes, depending on the size of the fish, until the flesh just flakes. Baste the fish with the cooking liquid several times during cooking. Serve immediately.

Serves: 6

Big Ma's Barbecued Salmon

Equipment:
Paper towels
Small paring knife
Glass baking dish

Ingredients:
6 salmon steaks
1 lemon
Salt to taste
Freshly ground pepper to taste
1 cup barbecue sauce

Directions:

- Wash the fish and pat dry with paper towels. Place the fish in the glass baking dish and sprinkle with salt and pepper. Squeeze the lemon over the fish, turning to cover.
- Place the fish over hot charcoal and grill

4 to 5 minutes per side. As you remove the fish, brush on the barbecue sauce. Cover the baking dish and allow the fish to sit for several minutes.

Serves: 6

SIDE DISHES

Gum-Gum's Corn Pudding

Equipment:
Large cast-iron skillet
Medium cooking knife
Large mixing bowl
Long-handled wooden spoon
2-quart glass casserole
Large baking pan

Ingredients:
6 ears corn, shucked
1 stick butter
$1/4$ cup finely chopped onion
3 large eggs
2 tbsp. sugar
1 tsp. salt
$1/4$ tsp. freshly ground pepper
$1/2$ tsp. nutmeg
$1/2$ tsp. vanilla extract
1 cup milk
1 cup light cream or half-and-half

Directions:

- Cut the kernels off the ears of corn.
- In the large skillet, melt the butter. Add the onion and sauté 5 minutes. Add the corn and sauté gently 5 minutes.
- Preheat oven to 350°. Meanwhile, mix together the eggs, sugar, salt, pepper, nutmeg, and vanilla extract. Fold in the corn mixture. Add the milk and light cream or half-and-half. Mix well until smooth. Butter the inside of the casserole and pour in the corn mixture.
- Place the casserole in the large baking pan and pour in enough water to come about halfway up the casserole. Place in the oven and bake 45 minutes to 1

hour, until the corn is set.

Serve: 6 to 8

Garlic Mashed Potatoes

Equipment:
Vegetable peeler
Medium-size knife
Large pot
Potato masher
Fork

Ingredients:
6 large baking potatoes
3 sticks butter
1 tsp. salt freshly ground pepper to taste
6 cloves garlic, finely chopped
$1/4$ cup half-and-half

Directions:

- Peel the potatoes. Cut into eighths. Place in the pot and cover with water. Bring to a boil. Reduce the flame a little and boil gently 20 minutes, or until just fork-tender.
- Drain off the water; immediately add the butter and begin to mash the potatoes. You can add more butter as you go along. (We like ours rich and buttery.) Add the salt and a generous grinding of pepper. Add the garlic and continue mashing until the potatoes become smooth. Add the half-and-half and beat with a fork until smooth again.

Serves: 6 to 8

Holiday Sweet-potato Fries

Equipment:
Large pot
Small paring knife
Large cast-iron skillet
Long-handled slotted spoon
Small mixing bowl
Paper towels

Ingredients:
6 sweet potatoes

$^1/_2$ cup packed brown sugar
2 tsp. salt
$^1/_2$ tsp. nutmeg
$^1/_2$ tsp. cinnamon
1 cup all-purpose flour
Vegetable oil for frying

Directions:

- Place the sweet potatoes in a large pot. Cover with water and place over a high flame. When the pot comes to a boil, reduce the flame and cook, gently boiling until you can just pierce the potatoes with a fork. Drain the potatoes and allow them to cool.
- When the potatoes are cool, peel them. Cut the potatoes into slices about $^1/_2$ inch thick. Cut the slices as you would for French fries.
- In a small bowl, mix together the brown sugar, 1 tsp. salt, the nutmeg, and cinnamon. Set aside.
- Mix together the flour and 1 tsp. of salt. Dredge the potatoes in the flour. Heat 2 inches of vegetable oil in a large skillet. When the oil is hot, add the potatoes. Fry until golden brown. Fry the potatoes in batches. Drain on paper towels and sprinkle with the sugar mixture.

Serves: 6 to 8

Classic Macaroni and Cheese

Equipment:

Large saucepan
Small saucepan
Small whisk
Fork
2-qt. casserole

Ingredients:

3 qt. water
1 tsp. salt
1 lb. short macaroni
8 tbsp. butter
4 tbsp. all-purpose flour
2$^1/_2$ cups evaporated milk
2 eggs, beaten
1$^1/_2$ lb. sharp cheddar cheese, grated

1 tsp. paprika
$^1/_2$ cup bread crumbs

Directions:

- Bring the water to a boil in a large saucepan. Add the salt; then add the macaroni, stirring constantly so it does not stick. Cook 10 to 12 minutes, until just done. Drain under cool water and set aside.
- Preheat the oven to 350°.
- Melt 6 tbsp. of butter in the saucepan. Whisk in the flour. Cook, stirring constantly, for about 1 minute. Remove from stove. Slowly add the evaporated milk. Allow this mixture to cool, then add the beaten eggs.
- Use the 2 tbsp. of butter to grease the 2-qt. casserole. Add a layer of macaroni, then a layer of cheese. Continue until the casserole is full. Pour the milk mixture over and sprinkle with extra cheese, the paprika, and the bread crumbs.
- Bake in the preheated oven 30 to 45 minutes, until brown and bubbly.

Serves: 6 to 8

Sweet-potato-stuffed Apples

Equipment:

Large pot
Small paring knife
Wooden spoon
Small spoon
Baking pan
Cutting board

Ingredients:

4 medium-size sweet potatoes
6 tbsp. butter
4 tbsp. brown sugar
$^1/_2$ tsp. salt
$^1/_2$ tsp. freshly ground black pepper
4 red Delicious apples
1 lemon
16 whole cloves
Ground cinnamon
2 marshmallows, cut in half

Directions:

- Preheat oven to 325°.
- Place the potatoes, unpeeled, in a large pot and cover with water. Bring to a boil, lower flame, and cook until the potatoes can be easily pierced with a fork. Drain the potatoes.
- As soon as the potatoes are cool enough to handle, peel them. Mash the potatoes in a large bowl and add the butter, brown sugar, salt, and pepper.
- Cut off the top of the apples and scoop out the centers, leaving about $^1/_4$ inch of skin and flesh. Squeeze the lemon juice into the apples and around the sides.
- Stick 4 cloves into each apple. Fill the apples with the potato mixture. Sprinkle the top with cinnamon.
- Place the apples in a baking pan and place in preheated oven. Bake 15 minutes. Top each apple with a marshmallow half and return to oven. Bake until the topping is brown.

Serves: 4

Rice with Raisins

Equipment:

Large heavy saucepan with top
Long-handled cooking fork
Wooden cooking spoon

Ingredients:

2 tbsp. butter
1 cup long-grain white rice
2 cups boiling water
1 small cinnamon stick
$^1/_2$ tsp. ground turmeric
$^1/_2$ tsp. Bijol (see Note)
1 tsp. salt
$^3/_4$ cup seedless golden raisins
1 tsp. sugar

Directions:

- Heat the saucepan over medium flame, and add the butter. When fully melted and slightly foaming, add the rice and stir until well coated. Do not let the rice brown.
- Add the water, cinnamon stick, turmeric, Bijol, and salt. Bring immediately to a boil and cover.

- Reduce the flame to very low and cook 15 to 20 minutes, until all the water has been absorbed.
- Remove the rice from the stove and discard the cinnamon stick. Add the raisins and sugar. Stir to mix well. Cover and let sit until ready to serve.

Serves: 4

Note: Bijol is a brand of achiote powder, a seasoning made from annato (a seed from the Yucatan), used to make yellow rice and available in most Mexican and Hispanic markets.

Celebration Spinach

Equipment:
Small paring knife
Large casserole with cover
Long-handled wooden spoon
Salad spinner
Cutting board

Ingredients:
3 lb. spinach, well washed
2 tbsp. olive oil
3 cloves garlic, finely chopped
1 cup shiitake mushroom slices (tops only)
$1/2$ tsp. red pepper flakes
1 tsp. balsamic vinegar

Directions:
- Pick over the spinach, removing all tough stems. Wash several times in cold water, to remove all sand and grit. Spin in salad spinner to remove water.
- Heat the oil in a large casserole. Add the garlic and cook 2 minutes. Add the mushrooms and sauté 5 minutes. Add the spinach and cover. Cook 2 minutes.
- Uncover, stir, and toss; cover again and cook several minutes more until wilted.
- Drain off all of the liquid; add the red pepper flakes and the balsamic vinegar. Toss to coat.

Serves: 4

South Side Okra and Tomatoes

Equipment:
Small paring knife
Cutting board
Large cast-iron skillet
Wooden spoon

Ingredients:
$1^1/2$ lb. fresh okra
2 tbsp. olive oil
$1/2$ cup thinly sliced onion
$1^1/2$ cups seeded and coarsely chopped tomatoes
4 cloves garlic, finely chopped
1 tsp. thyme
1 tsp. salt
Freshly ground pepper to taste
Pinch red pepper flakes
1 cup cooked corn kernels (optional)

Directions:
- Wash the okra. Trim the ends, as needed.
- Heat the olive oil in the skillet. Add the onions and cook 2 minutes. Add the okra and cook gently 5 minutes. Add the tomatoes, garlic, thyme, salt, pepper, red pepper flakes, and, if desired, corn. Stir to mix well and distribute the seasonings. Cook 10 to 15 minutes more. Check seasonings.

Serves: 4

DESSERTS

Aunt M's Peach Cobbler

Equipment:
Small paring knife
Cutting board
Medium-size glass mixing bowl
Small mixing bowl
Deep-dish glass baking dish
Rolling pin
Long-handled cooking spoon

Ingredients:
8 large ripe peaches, peeled, pitted, and sliced
1 tsp. lemon juice
1 cup sugar
4 tbsp. all-purpose flour
1 tsp. nutmeg
$1/4$ tsp. cinnamon
Pastry for a two-crust pie
4 tbsp. butter
3 tbsp. water
2 drops almond extract

Directions:
- Peel, pit, and slice the peaches. Sprinkle with lemon juice and turn to coat. Mix together the sugar, flour, nutmeg, and cinnamon.
- Preheat oven to 450°.
- Line the bottom and sides of a deep-dish glass baking pan with the piecrust. Add the peaches, alternating between them and the sugar-spice mixture, until the baking dish is full. Dot the top with pads of butter. Sprinkle with water to which the almond flavor has been added.
- Top the dish with a layer of piecrust. Crimp the edges closed and trim. Slash the top with a knife for airholes. Sprinkle the top with additional nutmeg and cinnamon.
- Bake 10 minutes. Reduce the heat to 350° and bake 30 to 40 minutes, until the top is golden brown with juices bubbling out.

Serves: 6 to 8

Note: For this recipe, we use Jiffy or Pillsbury piecrust mix.

Ginger Fried Bananas

Equipment:
Small paring knife
Cutting board
Large cast-iron skillet
Spatula
Ice-cream scoop

When you make a dish that looks delicious, everybody wants to eat it. That's why it's good to take your time during preparation. South Side Okra and Tomatoes, a classic African American vegetable medley, is easy to make and beautiful to present.

Dessert time can be delightful at family gatherings, especially when you have unusual treats to offer those gathered. Brainstorm with your children to see what ideas they have for menu items. These Sweet-Potato–Stuffed Apples actually serve as vegetable and dessert in one!

Ingredients:

4 bananas (firm but ripe)
3 tbsp. butter
2 tbsp. light brown sugar
1 tbsp. finely chopped peeled fresh ginger
Vanilla ice cream

Directions:

- Peel the bananas and cut them in half lengthwise. Cut each piece in half crosswise, yielding four pieces per banana.
- Melt the butter in the skillet over a medium flame. Add the brown sugar and stir to melt, about 20 seconds. Add the ginger and cook, stirring constantly, until the ginger becomes fragrant and begins to color, about 30 seconds.
- Add the bananas, sliced side down. Cook until lightly browned on one side, about 1 minute. Turn and cook 1 minute more.
- Transfer the bananas to a plate, scraping up as much of the caramelized ginger as possible. Serve with vanilla ice cream.

Serves: 4

Fresh Fruit Mango Sorbet

Equipment:

Small paring knife
Cutting board
Electric blender
Large glass mixing bowl
Fork

Ingredients:

4 large ripe mangoes
1 lime
1 juice orange
1 cup sugar
1 cup water

Directions:

- Peel the mangoes and cut the meat from the seed; coarsely chop and place in the bowl of a blender. Add the juice of 1 lime and 1 juice orange. Add the sugar and water.
- Pulse the blender until you get a thick mixture. Taste and add more sugar to taste. Pulse to liquefy. Pour into the glass mixing bowl.
- Place in the freezer. Allow to set 1 to 2 hours (depending on your freezer), stirring every 10 to 15 minutes so that it does not freeze into a solid block but rather into a cold delicious sorbet (thick slush).

Serves: 4 to 6

Oatmeal·Raisin·and· Cranberry Bars

Equipment:

Large mixing bowl
Long-handled wooden spoon
Glass baking dish (9 x 13 inches)

Ingredients:

2 sticks butter, softened
1 cup packed brown sugar
$1/2$ cup granulated sugar
3 eggs
1 tsp. vanilla extract
$1/2$ tsp. almond extract
$1 1/2$ cups all-purpose flour
1 tsp. baking powder
1 tsp. ground cinnamon
$1/2$ tsp. salt
3 cups uncooked old-fashioned oats
1 cup golden raisins
1 cup dried cranberries

Directions:

- Preheat oven to 350°.
- Grease the glass baking dish.
- Melt the butter and fold together with the sugars in the mixing bowl. Add the eggs, vanilla, and almond extract. Mix well.
- Combine the flour, baking powder, cinnamon, and salt. Fold into the butter and sugar. Mix well. Add the oats, raisins, and cranberries. Mix well.
- Fold the mixture into the greased 9 x13-inch baking dish. Using the back of a spoon, push the mixture around to distribute evenly and press down to pack.
- Bake 10 to 15 minutes. Allow to cool. Cut into squares or oblongs.

Serves: Approximately 18 bars per pan

North Star Sugar Cookies

Equipment:

Flour sifter
Saucepan
Wooden spoon
Rolling pin
Cookie cutters
Baking sheet
Wire cooling rack

Ingredients:

4 cups all-purpose flour, sifted
2 tsp. baking powder
1 tsp. salt
3 sticks butter, softened
2 cups granulated sugar
3 tsp. vanilla extract
3 eggs, beaten

Directions:

- Sift together the flour, baking powder, and salt. Melt the butter and add the sugar and vanilla. When cool, add the eggs. Slowly mix in the flour mixture, blending to make a smooth dough.
- Preheat oven to 375°.
- Roll the dough out on a lightly floured surface to about $1/8$-inch thickness. Cut with a cookie cutter into stars, trees, etc. Reroll and cut trimmings.
- Bake on a lightly greased cookie sheet 8–10 minutes, until pale tan. Transfer to a rack to cool. Sprinkle with additional sugar.

Makes: 7 dozen

Rum Cake à la Stephanie

Equipment:

Bundt pan
Cooking spray
Large mixing bowl
Electric mixer
Saucepan
Rubber mixing spoon
Skewer

Ingredients:

1/2 cup cold water
1/3 cup cooking oil
3 eggs
4 tablespoons rum extract
18-oz. box yellow cake mix with pudding
1 cup chopped walnuts

Ingredients for glaze:

1 stick butter
1/4 cup water
1 cup granulated sugar
3 tbsp. rum extract

Directions:

- Preheat oven to 325°.
- Spray bundt pan with cooking spray.
- In mixing bowl, blend water, oil, eggs, and rum extract. Blend thoroughly.
- Add cake mix. Blend until smooth.
- Scatter walnuts in bottom of bundt pan.
- Pour batter into bundt pan.
- Bake until done, 35 to 45 minutes. Toothpick should come out clean. Do not overcook.
- Allow it to cool, approximately 15 to 20 minutes.
- Put cake plate on top of bundt pan. Turn with bundt pan on top. After about 3 minutes, pan should easily slide off cake.
- Allow to cool for 10 minutes.

Glaze

- In medium-size saucepan, melt butter. Stir in water and sugar.
- Boil for 5 minutes.
- Remove from heat and stir in rum extract.
- Use a skewer and insert into cake to make small holes.
- Spoon glaze on top of cake and allow it to seep into holes. Allow glaze to drip down sides of cake.

BEVERAGES

Tropical Sorrel Punch

Equipment:

Very large pot (3 gallons) with top
Vegetable peeler
Small paring knife
Cutting board
Long-handled wooden spoon
Strainer

Ingredients:

2 gallons water
1 lb. fresh ginger
2 oranges
2 packages dried sorrel (about 10 oz., total)
8 cloves
2 lb. sugar or more to taste
Fresh mint for garnish

Directions:

- In a large pot, bring the water to a boil.
- Peel the ginger and slice into rounds. Peel the skin off the oranges.
- When the water boils, add the sorrel, ginger, orange peel, and cloves. Boil 5 minutes. Remove from heat. Cover tightly and allow the pot to sit for several days. Stir occasionally.
- After several days, strain the liquid and add sugar to taste.
- Serve in tall glasses with ice, garnished with sprig of mint.

Serves: Many

Iced Tea Punch

Equipment:

Large pot
Long-handled spoon
Large glass pitcher
Tall glasses

Ingredients:

16 cups water (1 gallon)
8 tea bags
2-inch piece cinnamon stick
6 cloves
1 1/2 cups sugar, or more to taste
1 can frozen orange-juice concentrate
1 can frozen-lemonade concentrate
Fresh mint for garnish

Directions:

- In a large pot, bring the water to a boil. Add the tea bags, cinnamon stick, and cloves. Remove from stove. Let tea steep 15 minutes. Remove the tea bags, cinnamon, and cloves. Stir in sugar and orange juice and lemonade concentrates. Set aside to cool.
- When cool, pour into pitchers and refrigerate until cold.
- Serve in tall glasses with ice, garnished with a sprig of mint.

Serves: 12

Many mothers make special cakes for the holidays that loved ones remember all year long. What's your special cake that you can make with your family? Here's Rum Cake à la Stephanie—my sister—that she makes for the adults. She makes a second cake without rum for the children.

document your events

SO MANY SPECIAL MOMENTS OCCUR WHEN LOVED ONES GET TOGETHER. AS TIME GOES· BY, IT'S HARD TO REMEMBER everything. That's why documenting your activities is so important. Plus, you can have lots of fun later using the fruits of your documentary efforts to share your experiences with everyone. You can include pictures on a family lineage Web site. You can e-mail photos to loved ones all over the country. Why not make a compilation reel of great moments from the year's activities that you documented with your video camera? You can make screen savers with your favorite shots. And you can send out an audiocassette with tidbits of different people's wishes for each other. The options are incredible. Once you have the raw material—images and memories of your own family—your creativity can lead you to so many ways to package those memories.

Take Pictures

Photographs are priceless ways to capture great moments. What's more, everybody can participate in picture taking. All you need is a little bit of preparation and planning in order to be able to take great pictures at every family function. Here are some suggestions to get you started:

- Know your camera and how to operate it. Read the instruction manual carefully before you head out to your event.
- If necessary, make a cheat sheet for how to operate the camera that you carry with you.

- Bring extra film so that you can take lots of pictures. The more pictures you take, the better chance you have of getting great ones.
- Make sure your batteries are fresh. Bring extras too, for your camera and flash.
- Take your time. Shots that are well thought out will always look better.
- Think before you shoot. What do you want the shot to look like? Plan your shot.
- Fill the frame. Move in so that your family or the scene fills the whole frame.

- Concentrate on the picture.
- Don't be afraid to experiment. Try different angles and shoot in different kinds of light. For example, shoot into the sun while using a flash. Or shoot with the sun at your back. When you're inside, always use your flash.
- Shoot when your family members are involved in activities, not just when they know you are taking a picture or are posing.
- Write the names and dates on the back of your pictures as well as the event and any notes you might wish to recall later.

- If you're having a party or event, buy disposable cameras and pass them around. And don't forget to give them to the children. Show them how to operate the cameras, and then see what great images they capture.
- Shoot with the camera held both vertically and horizontally.
- Make sure you always hold the camera steady.

Videotape Your Festivities

Nearly every family has access to a video camera these days. What better way to document your family's evolution than with a moving picture! This is a great activity for teens who want to have something active to do or for another family member who is observant and persistent.

Learn to Use the Camera

As with still pictures, it's important to have a good sense of how to use a video camera before you venture out to document an event.

- Read the instructions carefully. Parents can take time to teach children and teens in advance about the different features and capabilities of the camera.
- Practice making videos at home to master handling the camera and keeping it still.
- Learn how to attach your camera to a tripod for longer interviews. This makes it possible to set your camera down on a table or other surface, so you don't have to hold it. It also keeps the camera completely still.

Shoot Your Event

Make sure you arrive with your video camera, several 60- or 90-minute videotapes, extra batteries, and a tripod.

- Before taking any pictures, survey the landscape. If you are outside, look for anything that marks the boundaries of the space, such as a banner for a family reunion. Notice the different activities that are underway.
- When you start filming, take your time and hold the camera steady. Videotaping can get a bit wobbly if you move quickly.
- Begin with a close-up that provides reference for your activity; then zoom out to a larger view of the scene. Move your camera slowly from left to right to take in the whole scene.
- If your camera records sound, narrate as you go along. Say your name, the date, and exactly where you are. Describe what you are seeing as you take in the scenery. As you notice people through your camera lens, say who they are and what their relationship is to you. Invite them to say something as well.
- Pause in your filming by using the pause button. Whenever you want to stop and look, pause rather than stopping the camera. This will make your film easier to view later.
- Pay attention to what's happening. Some things are better for filming than others. For instance, people standing and posing in front of the camera is not exciting for the moving pictures that video cameras make. The video camera loves activity, such as sporting events, plays, songs, narration. You can capture everything from your grandmother rocking in her chair to toddlers taking their first steps.
- Notice who is present. Be sure to touch base with each group of people. You can invite them to say something about the event or your family. Always ask them to say their names.
- Get someone to assist you. That person can be the interviewer, encouraging people to share stories about the family and tidbits about their lives now.
- When you get to older people, give yourself more time. They like to tell stories that often last a little longer. As they are talking, zoom in and out.

Notice what's interesting about their environment and about them. If your great-aunt is shucking corn while talking, zoom in on her hands as she speaks. In this way, your film will be more dynamic.
- Videotape the food and table settings before people start eating. Be sure to show the people who are preparing the food. You can ask them about the menu and how they prepared certain dishes that look great.

Use a Tape Recorder

It may seem old-fashioned to some folks, but I love tape recorders. Without too much intrusion, you can turn on a recorder and get great interviews from people. The most important thing to remember when you use a tape recorder is to place the mouthpiece close enough to the speaker so that the sound comes through clearly.

- Test your tape recorder before you leave home. Put in a new tape and batteries and record a few words. Listen for the sound quality.
- Set your volume at a midpoint, such as number 5. In this way you can adjust higher or lower later, depending upon the clarity of the sound you are able to capture.
- Before you record, let your family know what you're doing.
- Speak to people individually rather than in a group. You will get better sound.
- Make sure that people state their names clearly.

The Creative Team

Writer	Harriette Cole
Photographer	John Pinderhughes
Recipes	John Pinderhughes
Book Designer	Gregory Gray, Little Gray House
Book Design Assistants	Mark Rangel, Carlos Visintine
Fashion Stylist	Lois Barrett
Photographer's Assistants	Isaac Diggs, Bayete Ross-Smith
Fashion Resources	Nigerian Fabrics and Fashions, Moshood, Cassandra Bromfield, 4W Circle, Brooklyn, New York
Makeup and Hair Stylists	Doris "Brazil" Kent, Larry Johnson
Craft Stylists	Ghenet Pinderhughes, Tiffany Hasborne, Bebe Granger Cuyjet, Christina Carr
Prop Stylists	Sharon Pendana, Jamiyl Young
Food Stylist	Melanee Harvin for Mel's Fork
Cake Design	Charmaine Jones, Isn't That Special Outrageous Cakes
Cover Shot Location	Michael Cooper/Cooper Branding
Editorial Assistants/ Researchers	Tanesha Barnes-Diallo, Andrea Hillhouse, Agunda Okeyo, Christina Peppers, Julius Robins, Subira Shaw, Shalea Walker, Nadia Symister, Jamiyl Young, Marsha Ganthier
Editorial Support	Victoria Benning, Cindi Cook
Research Support at Camp Atwater	Henry Thomas, Dee Thomas, Wanda Johnson, Monikka Stallworth, and the wonderful children who shared their wisdom so generously
Other Research Support	Tracie Howard, Cee Cee Coppedge

We Thank You

When I was a little girl my mother and grandmother used to tell my sisters and me all the time, "You don't do anything by yourself, girls." They were right. Most every effort is a collective one. Many visible and behind-the-scenes hands participate in supporting and making possible just about everything we do. In African tradition, this awareness extends to the ancestors whose efforts have paved the way for us to follow. Knowing this, John and I want to offer our deepest gratitude to all who helped to make this project possible.

The Photo Subjects

The Cover: Al Cuyjet, Alyssa Cuyjet; Fatouseck Rahman, Henrí Heard; Larry Carr, Christina Clements Carr, Millie Clements, Ashley Carr, Cameron Carr; Charles Lloyd Pinderhughes; Deneen Moulden, Lauren Offer, Perez Mackell, Antonia Harris

Kwanzaa Celebration and Naming Ceremony: Aissatou Bey-Grecia, Billy Ali Seck, Akhnaten Spencer-El, Mojisola Alawode-El, Lemuria Alawode-El, Hanabel McDuffy

Kwanzaa Naming Ceremony for Sahar Gray: Terri Wisdom, Myrtle Duncan Hamilton, Harrold Hamilton, Maya Jones, Nkosi Gray, Sahar Gray, Wayne Duncan, Robin Duncan Brooks, Obataiye Brooks, Ayinde Brooks, Oliver Gray, Rhonda Hamilton, Ali Wisdom

Kwanzaa Celebration: E. Lee White Bembury, Charmane Bembury, Salehe Bembury, Abeje Bembury, Leslie Jean-Bart, Sienna Pinderhughes

Kwanzaa Dance Performance: Wali and Koumba Rahman Ndiaye, Artistic Directors, Drum and Spirit of Africa Society; Obara Wali Rahman, Andara, and the incredible performers young and older

Creative Projects: Harambee Center for Youth and Community Service, Danbury, Connecticut, William Curtis, Julie Barnes, and the creative children

Naming Ceremony for Cameron Michael Fane: Lana Turner, Michael William Fane, Eric Michael Fane, Valecia Ambrose, Rev. Calvin O. Butts, Parker McAllister, and family and friends

The Matthews and Scott Family Reunion: Lucille Matthews Brown, Laureen Offer, Dr. Brenda Scott Brown, Bernice Brown, and all the members of the Matthews–Scott 2000 Family Reunion

Christmas Festivities in Baltimore: Doris F. Cole, Stephanie Hill, Kori-Morgan Hill, Cole-Stephen Hill, Patricia Branch, Delvin Branch, Myrtle Cole, and other members of the Cole and Branch families and friends

Grandfather and Granddaughter at Christmas: George Lopez and Raisa Rhoden

The Jack and Jill Christmas Carolers: Ghenet Pinderhughes, Brook Smith, Jessica Douglas, and Jonathan Geffrard

Christmas Tree-Trimming and other Activities: Larry Carr, Christina Clements Carr, Ashley Carr, Cameron Carr, and Marlowe Williams; black angel tree topper by Sauda (Arline Billbrough and Joanne Harris)

Holiday Lights: Gwyneth and Jeff Shick in Palm Bay, Florida, for sharing their spectacular decorations with us, and Kyle and Cynthia Divincenvo in snowy New Jersey

Christmas and Kwanzaa: Al Cuyjet, Beverly Granger Cuyjet, Allysa Cuyjet

Kwanzaa and Family Reunions: Victoria Pinderhughes, Ghenet Pinderhughes, Sienna Pinderhughes, and the entire Pinderhughes clan, and the Calvert County, Maryland, family reunion

Family Reunion Photos: Rose Marcel, Marie Therese Mith, Ronald Mith, Damali Mith, Allison Mith, Marie Joelle Mith-Joseph, Stan Joseph, Rose Marline Charles, Nicholas Charles, Tiffany Rose Charles, Richard Mith, Naomi Mith, Shandon Mith, Serge Ganthier, Nadine Ganthier, Andrew Ganthier

Slumber Party Photos: Alana Bowers, Caron Mullins, Chelsea Owings, Curtira Williams, Takayla Wilson, Deniah Mitchell, Kabria Haskins, Kori-Morgan Hill

Other Photo Subjects: McKenzie C. Hayes, Pam Hayes, and the many smiling faces seen throughout the book

Additional Images: Map illustration—Anne Smith; Marcus Garvey, Sojourner Truth, Malcolm X, Paul Robeson, Harriet Tubman, Nat Turner, Hank Aaron, Toni Morrison, Sidney Poitier, Ralph Ellison, Thurgood Marshall, Dr. Ben Carson, Martin Luther King, Jr., Shirley Chisholm, and James Baldwin—Getty Images; Zora Neale Hurston—Corbis; Florida Christmas decorations—George Chinsee; family photos—courtesy of the families

Special Thanks
We would like to offer special thanks to Madeleine Morel, agent extraordinaire, for helping to make this book possible. We'd also like to thank Andrea Davis Pinkney, who first saw the vision of this project, and Wendy Lefkon, who held our hand through every page of the production. Gregory Gray deserves a medal for wading through the many images and design challenges that presented themselves. Thanks also to Elliott Kreloff for supporting the design process to its completion, and Jody Revenson, Alexander Eiserloh, and Christopher Caines for so diligently bringing up the rear.

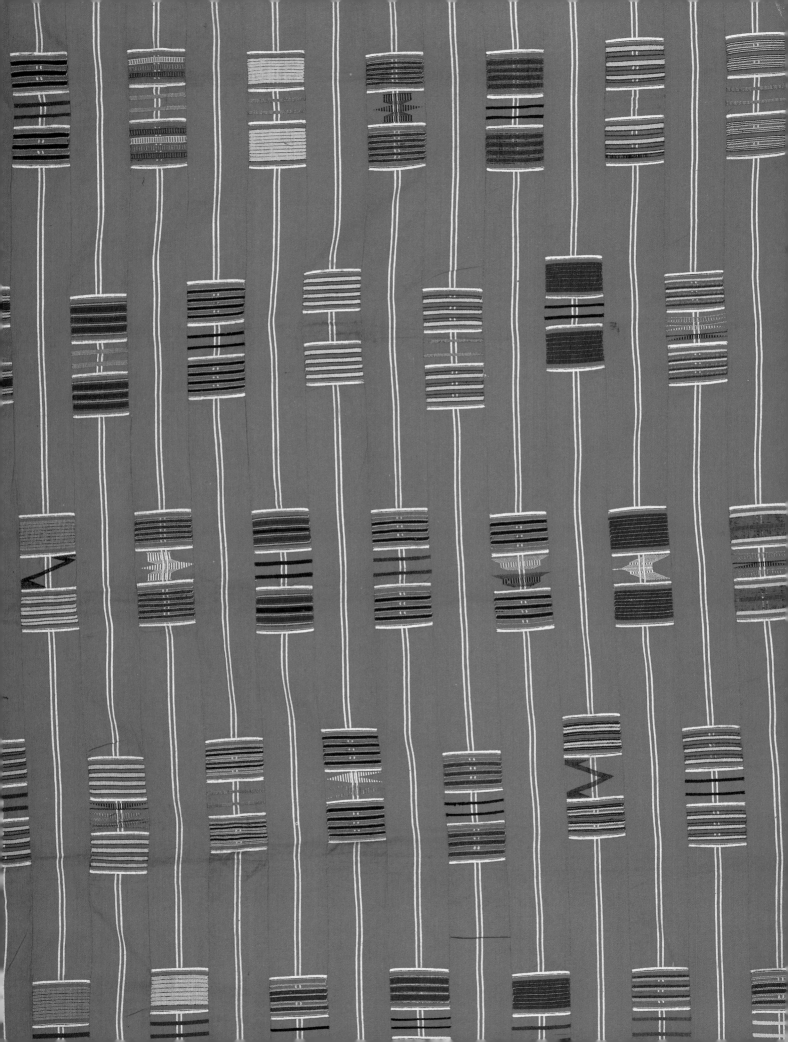